W9-BNL-976

asís

INSIGHT COMPACT GUIDE

CUBa

Compact Guide: Cuba is the ultimate quick-reference guide to this popular Caribbean destination. It tells you all you need to know about the island's attractions, from the colonial splendour of Havana to the intimate charms of Trinidad, from the heights of the Sierra Maestra to the languid pleasures of the coast.

This is one of 133 Compact Guides, combining the interests and enthusiasms of two of the world's best known information providers: Insight Guides, whose titles have set the standard for visual travel guides since 1970, and Discovery Channel, the world's premier source of nonfiction television programming.

Discovery
CHANNEL

APA PUBLICATIONS

Part of the Langenscheidt Publishing Group

Insight Compact Guide: Cuba

Written by: Beate Schümann
English version by: Paul Fletcher
Photography by: Glyn Genin
Additional photography by: Fred Mawer (pages 24 and 81);
  Anna Mockford and Nick Bonnetti (pages 6, 91 and 94)
Cover picture by: Angelo Cavalli/Getty Images
Picture Editor: Hilary Genin
Maps: Polyglott Verlag

Editorial Director: Brian Bell
Managing Editor: Tony Halliday

CONTACTING THE EDITORS: As every effort is made to provide accurate information in this publication, we would appreciate it if readers would call our attention to any errors and omissions by contacting:
Apa Publications, PO Box 7910, London SE1 1WE, England.
Fax: (44 20) 7403 0290
e-mail: insight@apaguide.co.uk

Information has been obtained from sources believed to be reliable, but its accuracy and completeness, and the opinions based thereon, are not guaranteed.

© 2004 APA Publications GmbH & Co. Verlag KG Singapore Branch, Singapore.

First Edition 2001; Updated 2004
Printed in Singapore by Insight Print Services (Pte) Ltd
Original edition © Polyglott-Verlag Dr Bolte KG, Munich

Worldwide distribution enquiries:
APA Publications GmbH & Co. Verlag KG (Singapore Branch)
38 Joo Koon Road, Singapore 628990
Tel: (65) 6865-1600, Fax: (65) 6861-6438

Distributed in the UK & Ireland by:
GeoCenter International Ltd
The Viables Centre, Harrow Way, Basingstoke,
Hampshire RG22 4BJ
Tel: (44 1256) 817987, Fax: (44 1256) 817-988

Distributed in the United States by:
Langenscheidt Publishers, Inc.
46–35 54th Road, Maspeth, NY 11378
Tel: (1 718) 784-0055, Fax: (1 718) 784-0640

www.insightguides.com

CUBa

Introduction

Places

Culture

Travel Tips

△ **Botanical Gardens (p63)** A huge collection of flora from all over the world can be seen here, including 285 types of palm tree.

▽ **El Morro (p77)** This fortress, built in the 17th century, has fine views over Santiago, the Sierra Maestra and the coast.

▷ **Viñales (p55)** Emerging from the flat Valle de Viñales are these huge, impressive *mogotes*, a series of limestone rocks about 400m (1,300ft) high. Nicknamed 'elephants' backs', they were created by erosion.

△ **Museo de la Revolución (p39)** Here you can follow the events leading to the Revolution, with life-sized sculptures of the *guerrilleros*, and even their blood-stained shirts on show.

◁ **Trinidad (p65)** A colonial gem of a town, conserved as a World Heritage Site, Trinidad has many fine buildings, such as this one on the Plaza Mayor, dating from the 18th century. At this time, the town prospered, with smuggling, sugar barons, slave traders and pirates all making their mark.

▽ **Cayo Largo (p96)**
This island offers long, sandy beaches, coral reefs for divers, and an unspoilt natural environment.

> **Old Havana (p33)**
A stunning collection of colonial-style houses occupy the historic, central quarter of Cuba's capital.

◁ **Cayo Levisa (p56)**
For a Caribbean experience, try this small coral cay; it's fairly inaccessible, so you'll have plenty of space on its fine, sandy beach.

▽ **Santa Clara (p69)**
A bronze statue of Che Guevara stands in the Plaza de la Revolución of Santa Clara. It was here that Che's men ambushed a train carrying government troops.

◁ **Sierra Maestra (p81)**
Cuba's highest mountain range, in the east of the island, is the site of many uprisings and rebellions. The stark, rough terrain was ideal for the guerrilla war which Fidel Castro started here in 1956.

Pearl of the Caribbean

Cuba is a dream destination. Columbus sailed westward across the Atlantic, hoping to find India and its pots of gold; pirates such as Henry Morgan chased Spanish galleons, laden with Inca and Aztec gold; and the naturalist, Alexander von Humboldt, amazed by the crystal clear seas, went on a botanical expedition around the island.

At the beginning of the 20th century, this Caribbean island was a tourist paradise on a par with Palm Beach or Nice. In the 1920s and 1930s, Cuba became a playground, a casino and a brothel for millionaires. Every day, 30 planes left Miami for Havana: the gangster Al Capone was a long-stay guest and the writer Ernest Hemingway drank and went fishing here. For most of the population, however, the brutal dictatorships of that era brought oppression and suffering.

The Revolution in the late 1950s put a stop to tourism. Only the political allies of Fidel Castro and Che Guevara received invitations. But after the collapse of the Soviet Union in 1991, economic disaster loomed and now the delights of Cuba are being vigorously promoted once more.

Although the economy is still depressed, tourism is a growth industry and bringing new hope to the inhabitants. The island's dazzling white beaches have lost none of their magnetic appeal, but a Cuban holiday is not just for beach lovers. The inshore waters are ideal for diving, and spectacular scenery and attractive colonial towns lie just inland.

Below: welcome to Cuba
Bottom: on the tourist trail

BEHIND THE SCENES

When the warm air blows over the skin, it is easy to imagine that life is nothing more than a colourful T-shirt and the rhythm of the rumba. But behind the idyllic seafront, life is certainly not a beach for ordinary Cubans. *Macheteros* spend their working day under a blazing sun harvesting the razor-edged sugar canes which shred the skin on their hands. The skills of the highly trained professional classes are very much in demand, but

Opposite: a taste of paradise at Cayo Levisa

Sugar Island
The fertile soil and warm but moist weather conditions provide the perfect conditions for plantations. In the valleys, the main crop is sugar, hence the term 'Sugar Island' which is sometimes used to describe Cuba.

Home from the fields

pay is so poor that many prefer to spend their time showing tourists around. There is strict rationing and the shelves of State-run shops seem bare to affluent visitors.

Cubans seem to swing between melancholia and *joie de vivre*. Even the long-standing economic difficulties do not undermine their determination to survive, and they have devised some ingenious survival techniques. Merriment is one, music another. The island of Cuba is a temptation and you should succumb to temptations – they may never be repeated.

SITUATION AND LANDSCAPE

Set alongside the American continent, the island of Cuba seems tiny, but compared with the dimensions of many European countries, Cuba, along with its islands, is actually a quite sizable nation. With an area of 114,524 sq km (44,206 sq miles), it is bigger than Portugal or Austria and is the largest of the Caribbean islands, measuring 1,250km (775 miles) from Cabo San Antonio, the westernmost point, to Punta de Quemados in the southeast. It is barely 35km (22 miles) at its narrowest point and 198km (122 miles) at its widest.

The German explorer Alexander von Humboldt compared the outline of the island to a crocodile. Nicolás Guillén, the Cuban national poet, preferred to liken the shape to a lizard – long and green. The lurking threat which reptiles pose fits perfectly with Cuba's geostrategic position: the 'crocodile' lies only 150km (93 miles) south of the American city of Miami. Its western tail guards both access routes to the Gulf of Mexico, namely the Yucatán Channel and the Straits of Florida. In the east, its sharp eyes watch over the Windward Passage between Cuba and Haiti, the main shipping route between the Atlantic and the Caribbean Sea, with the Panama Canal beyond. Cuba clearly occupies a key position and this partly explains why the colonial powers and the Americans have always been so interested in developments here.

A quarter of the country is mountainous. Pico Turquino, at just under 2,000m (6,500ft), is the highest point in the Sierra Maestra, the island's highest mountain range. Over 200 rivers, none of which is longer than 250km (155 miles), help to irrigate the land. Between the mountain ranges lie flat open landscapes, some gently undulating.

Also part of Cuba are the 3,061 sq-km (1,181 sq-mile) Isla de la Juventud (Isle of Youth) and over 4,000 mostly uninhabited islands and coral cays or *cayos*. The countless reefs that lie close to the shore have proved extremely hazardous for sea captains, but for pirates, and now divers, they have proved to be goldmines in the true sense.

Mangrove forests cover broad stretches of the southern coastline, especially in the swampy areas of the Zapata Peninsula. Everywhere along the 5,700-km (3,500-mile) coastline lie rocky bays with idyllic beaches, lonely caves and sheer cliffs.

The white sandy beaches of Cuba are world famous, with the long shores of Varadero in the north perhaps the best known. A number of the other 300 other lesser-known beaches are also fabulous, including those of the islands, such as Cayo Largo and Cayo Coco. Amateur sailors and deep-sea anglers appreciate the countless natural harbours. Often shaped like bottle necks, the narrow inlets provide good protection from storms and serve as sheltered anchorages.

Below: biking through the Sierra de los Organos
Bottom: exploring the islands

CLIMATE AND WHEN TO GO

Cuba lies on the fringes of the tropics, and its climate is influenced by the North Atlantic high pressure zone. There are two seasons: the hot, sultry, but rainy 'summer' (May to October) and the dry 'winter' from November to April. January is the coolest month, with temperatures around 23°C (73°F), and it is hottest in July (30°C/86°F), although it is usually quite bearable in the shade of a tree. At night temperatures rarely drop below 20°C (68°F). In the Oriente, the east, it is always that little bit more sultry, hotter and drier.

The best time to visit Cuba is between December and March. Humidity and rainfall are high between May and November, although the rain usually comes in torrential showers. However, it is unusual for the sun to stay hidden behind the clouds all day. If you are intending to spend some time on the beach, don't be deceived by the fresh trade winds – they do not reduce the intensity of the sun.

When considering what clothes to take with you, remember that beachwear is not acceptable in churches, museums, restaurants and clubs. Although you will want plenty of light, cotton clothing, the cooling trade winds can bring rapid temperature changes. Air-conditioning systems are often set to low temperatures and you may then feel the need for a jumper or a jacket. It is

Below: shade at Playa Larga
Bottom: shells in the sand

advisable to pack some sort of light rainwear for the odd downpour.

HURRICANES

The meteorologists give them ordinary names, such as Kate, Andrew and Gordon, but these devastating cyclones have caused huge damage to the already battered Cuban economy.

When, in the autumn of 1985, hurricane Kate roared across the island at a speed of about 230kph (140mph), it destroyed a major part of the sugar crop. In 1992, Andrew wrecked the Government's ambitious food production plans and, instead of improved yields, the harvest fell well below the expected levels. In 1994, Gordon left a trail of destruction; in 1996 Lili struck, displacing thousands of people and ruining crops; and Mitch left untold damage in 1998. Hurricane Michelle in November 2001 hit hard, causing US$1.8bn damage, but 2002 was a particularly tough year for hurricanes. Hurricanes Isidore and then another Lili hit Western Cuba within 2 weeks (September/October) destroying much of the tobacco crop and many drying sheds, and causing 350,000 to be evacuated.

Hurricanes are the downside of the otherwise idyllic Caribbean weather. They usually occur between September and November, when the temperature of the sea and the air above it rises to 27°C (80°F) causing huge storm clouds to well up. The earth's rotation causes the clouds to swirl around at high speed and then to release large volumes of rain. As well as terrific wind damage, tidal waves cause flooding. The only consolation for the defenceless islanders is the well developed early warning system.

FLORA AND FAUNA

The whole of Cuba is sadly no longer as green as Nicolás Guillén's lizards. Much of the country's forest, comprising largely of pines, oaks and valuable hardwoods such as mahogany, fell victim to the needs of farmers and colonial planters

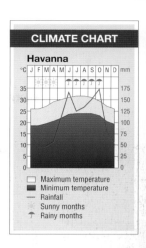

CLIMATE CHART

Havanna

- ☐ Maximum temperature
- ■ Minimum temperature
- — Rainfall
- ☀ Sunny months
- ☂ Rainy months

Banana crop

National tree

The royal palm, *palma real*, the national tree and native to the island, can reach a height of 40m (130ft). Everything from its roots to the tips of its leaves has a use. The 5-m (16-ft) long fronds are used as roofing material for the farmers' *bohíos* (huts) and the trunk is used to support the walls.

Below: the Soroa Forest
Bottom: the Cuban crocodile

in earlier centuries. Tobacco, pineapples and cassava were cultivated by the Indians, while coffee, bananas and sugar cane were brought in by the Spanish settlers. Densely wooded areas have survived only in the mountainous regions. In an effort to protect the island's fauna and flora, the Government has been carrying out an intensive reforestation programme.

Palm trees dominate the landscape of the interior. There are at least 30 different types of palms, including the coconut palm and the 'pregnant palm', known as *barrigona*, which is now a protected species growing only in Pinar del Río. Out of more than 8,000 different types of plants, one of the best known is the white, strongly scented national flower, the *mariposa* or butterfly flower, which is used to make a perfume of the same name.

The *tocororo* has been chosen as Cuba's national bird, mainly because its blue, red and white plumage is the same colour as the Cuban flag. In the fields, turkey vultures *(tiñosas)* and the white cattle egret, which often hitches a ride on the backs of cows, can be seen. Another common sight is the pelican diving for fish.

UNDER THREAT

The Cuban crocodile *(Crocodilus rhombifer)*, which survives on the Zapata Peninsula and the Isla de la Juventud, is being threatened with extinction. This is due to cross-breeding with the more numerous American crocodiles that enjoy the freshwater swamps as well. The mole-like, rat-sized, nocturnal *almiquí* is also under threat. Only a few of these insectivores remain in the eastern mountains.

No poisonous snakes or spiders live in Cuba, but the voracious mosquitoes that inhabit the wetlands can be very annoying. In the offshore waters, there is a fascinating display for divers in the range of corals, mussels and snails, not to mention the 900 or so species of tropical fish.

The slow pace of change that followed the Revolution has kept industrial pollution to a minimum, but out-of-date technology is highly pollutant. There is little investment in cleaner alternatives. However, the beaches are generally kept very clean, especially those in the main tourist areas.

THE CUBAN PEOPLE

More than 11 million people live on the island of Cuba. Population growth has been rapid – in 1953 the island supported a population of only 5.9 million. Despite great efforts to stem the pre-Revolutionary drift from the rural areas to the towns, many younger people continue to prefer to seek a full-time job in the urban areas than to carry out back-breaking chores in the plantations. About one fifth of Cubans live in the capital, Havana.

Below: good companions
Bottom: family values

A clear majority of Cubans are of European descent, mainly Spanish, with only a relatively small proportion having exclusively African roots. Immigration to this goldless colony did not start in earnest until the late 18th century. The newly independent United States of America wanted sugar in large quantities, but when the slaves revolted in Haiti,the previous supplier, 30,000 planters fled from Haiti to Cuba in 1795. The island soon became the main sugar exporter.

As the number of plantations increased, the demand for slaves grew dramatically and so

Demise of the Indians

When Cuba was discovered by Christopher Columbus in the 15th century, more than 100,000 Arawak-speaking Indigenous peoples – Taínos and Cíboneys – were living there. The Spanish colonists used them as slaves, exploiting them mercilessly in their frantic but unsuccessful search for gold. Within 50 years, most of the Indigenous people had been wiped out.

Below: enjoying the sun
Below: timeless Trinidad

Yorubas, Congos and Carabalís were bought in markets in the West African countries, in places like Nigeria, Senegal and Guinea. When Spain eventually abolished slavery in 1886 because it ceased to be economic, the major landowners turned to hiring 125,000 Chinese coolies on very restrictive contracts.

During the past 500 years, the various ethnic groups have intermarried and today 51 percent of Cubans are *mulattos* (mixed race), 37 percent are white, 11 percent black and about one percent Chinese. In order to put a stop to racial arrogance, Castro used to say that all Cubans were of mixed race. Racial discrimination is strictly forbidden.

IN EXILE

Just under 1 million Cubans live in exile in Florida. Most of these fled immediately after the Revolution or in 1980 and 1994 – when frustration with the politics and state of the economy peaked – often using spectacular methods of escape, such as roughly constructed rafts. In 1999 around 3,800 Cubans took to the Florida Straits, about 40 per cent of whom were picked up by the US coast guards – a six-year-old boy, Elian, was one, having lost his mother in the escape. After a long battle between Cuba and the US over

where he should live, he was eventually returned to Cuba in late 2000.

EDUCATION

Cuba prides itself on having a model education system. About a quarter of the State's budget goes to the schools and universities, so equality of opportunity, one of the main aims of the Revolution, can be realised. In 1959 some 24 percent of the population were illiterate, but a massive campaign has reduced this figure to 3 percent, a huge improvement when Cuba is compared to the rest of Latin America. Nevertheless, as with every other aspect of Cuban life, the education system has not escaped the severe strains imposed on it by the continuing economic crisis.

No Cuban leaves school without qualifications of some sort. Since 1977, attendance has been compulsory for all children from the age of five, and parents who do not send their children to school can be punished. Lessons last all day so that mothers can work.

The curriculum requires that every pupil must gain knowledge of agriculture, schools have vegetable plots. The aim of this policy is to bridge the divide between manual and non-manual workers. It also reinforces the point that education is a precious commodity and students must pay for it by serving the community.

Tobacco-rollers, mainly women, are among the best read in Cuba. While they are carrying out their monotonous work sitting on benches, rolling, cutting and sorting the tobacco leaves, a lector reads into a microphone Revolutionary texts, contemporary newspaper reports, poems and novels. Marx and Engels are the standard fare, but tear-jerking love stories are sometimes included.

HEALTH

Fidel Castro never used to appear in public without a fat Havana cigar, but in 1990 the world was taken by surprise when it was announced that he

Below: education is compulsory for all children
Bottom: at a market stall

had given up smoking, at least in public. As far as public health issues are concerned, the Cuban leader takes matters seriously and likes to be seen setting a good example.

A health service providing for every citizen from cradle to grave is one of the Government's finest achievements. Each district has a family doctor, the *médico de la familia*, who has 100–120 families to care for (the lowest doctor-patient ratio in the world). Everything from a common cold to cardiac complaints is treated free of charge. And the figures speak for themselves: child mortality fell to 7.27 percent in 2003 (compared to 6.69 percent in the US) and average life expectancy is an impressive 76–8 years. The Hermanos Almejeiras hospital in Havana is regarded as one of the best in Latin America.

The continuing economic crisis has taken its toll, of course. Frequent power cuts can affect operations, patients are sometimes asked to pay for medicines, and effective drugs may be in short supply, or only available for dollars or not at all. These shortages are often counterbalanced by the use of herbal medicines.

The population's calorie intake has fallen dramatically, and in 1992 the first cases of optic neuritis, inflammation of the optical nerve caused by nutritional deficiency, came to light. Thanks to the efficient health service, the problem was quickly nipped in the bud. But the greatest health problems are infectious diseases, heart and circulatory diseases and cancer. The incidence of Aids is slowly rising, though it is still low when compared to neighbours Haiti and Jamaica. Cuba's controversial but highly effective policy of creating HIV/AIDS sanatoriums has curbed the spread of the infection, which first made its appearance with soldiers returning from Angola in the 1980s.

Below: free health for all
Bottom: the herbal alternative

RELIGION

Although Roman Catholicism has been the national religion ever since the arrival of the Spaniards, only 38 percent of Cubans regard themselves as followers. Over half the population are described as non-believers, the rest are Protestants, and about 10,000 are Jews. Religious freedom is guaranteed by the Constitution, but incense and party membership are largely not compatible. Castro regards religion as the 'opium of the people' and has expelled priests and nuns from Cuba – for years the churches stood empty.

There now seems to have been a reconciliation between the Church and State. In 1988, Fidel Castro agreed to the importation of about 30,000 bibles, and in 1991 Christians were allowed to become members of the Communist Party. Now church congregations are growing larger, demonstrating that the Christian faith has survived despite an education system which promotes atheism. For dissidents, the church is regarded as the 'place of free thought'.

It is impossible to express in figures the proportion of the population who practise Afro-Cuban religions. They have their origins in black African society, but draw their followers from all racial groups, including whites. In times of hardship, the deities or *orishas* have more influence over Cuban lives than Castro's Politburo. The main sects are Santería *(see page 103)*, Palo Monte and Abakuá, and many would consider themselves followers of Santería and Catholicism.

The Pope's visit
In January 1998, Pope John Paul II visited Cuba, thereby confirming the Cuban government's abandonment of its earlier hostility to the Church and boosting the profile of Cuba in the eyes of Roman Catholics. But the visit had just as much political importance.

Castro said the visit showed Cuba had 'nothing to hide' from the world, and the Pope urged other countries to embrace Cuba; he sharply criticised trade sanctions maintained by the US against the island state.

As a gesture of goodwill, Castro allowed Christmas Day 1997 to be a public holiday for the first time since 1969, and since then it has been reinstated permanently.

A church altar

Below: bound for the market
Middle: fishing out of
Puerto Esperanza
Bottom: queues are common

THE ECONOMY

The disintegration of the Soviet Union in the early 1990s achieved something that a 40-year American embargo has been unable to do. When Cuba lost its main trading partner, the economy collapsed, as some 70 percent of the island's foreign trade was with Moscow and eastern Europe. Learning to live without the support of its political allies has proved to be a very painful experience for the Cuban government. Exports totalling 13 million tons have dwindled to 3.6 million tons. Sugar exports, once 80 percent of the country's total external trade, have fallen by a half since then.

OVERTURES TO INVESTORS

Along with massive cutbacks in expenditure, the gaping hole in the national accounts is being filled filled by the receipts from tourism, the export of nickel, fish, tobacco and citrus fruits. Although there are still shortages of some commodities, imports of oil from President Chavez's Venezuela have helped and public transport is running again, some factories have closed although others stagger on, and the shelves in the State-run shops are slowly filling up. However, if it had not been for the black market and neighbourhood support schemes, it would be difficult to imagine how the people would have survived.

However, after a few half-hearted reforms, the stubborn *caudillo* (leader) set about transforming an economic system based on centralised planning. There were no great fanfares to publicise the *volte face*, but for the first time foreign investors were wooed into creating joint venture schemes, with Spain, Canada and France among the main participants.

Tourism is, of course, Cuba's greatest hope for the future. Not only does it attract hard currency, it's also good PR. In September 1993, the Government introduced a law allowing self-employment in all manner of trades. Soap sellers and shoe repairers – that is, one-man operations with no employees – are now often in a better position financially than doctors and teachers, who are allowed to work only for the State. This ruling presents the Government with a difficult problem, but Castro does not want to put the nation's social achievements at risk.

DOLLAR POWER

Perhaps the most far-reaching measure to help the economy was the legalisation of the dollar in July 1993. This U-turn had a devastating effect on Cuba's core socialist beliefs. As wages paid in pesos are virtually worthless, anyone with relatives in Miami or who could persuade tourists to part with a few dollars was in a position to lead an extravagant lifestyle. Suddenly dollars started to emerge from under the floorboards, and it is now possible to buy virtually anything – although admittedly at prices the locals find extravagant.

The consequences are that when dollars are abundant among the privileged few, the tolerance of the rest of the populace, who have to endure serious shortages, is severely tested, and the solidarity engendered by common adversity has been fractured. Envy, frustration and anger are becoming increasingly evident among those denied access to the dollar economy. The State, which has the monopoly over currency dealing, is seen to be undermining the much-vaunted principle of equality. Castro wants capital but not capitalism.

Tourism's triumph
Tourism, once given a low priority in Fidel Castro's grand plan, is now the island's top industry, attracting much more hard currency than sugar. Even though Cuba is still officially off-bounds to Americans, around 2 million holiday-makers a year visit the island.

Below: joint venture
Bottom: dollar shop

The old Revolutionary's crisis managers are performing a balancing act without a safety net.

SUGAR

Every year, at the start of the sugar cane harvest in November, the rural population gathers for the *despedida de los macheteros*, the farewell ceremony for the cane cutters. Representatives of the Party, families and fellow villagers send off the 'nation's heroes' with music provided by brass bands and plenty of words of encouragement. The men who go off to perform the back-breaking work among the canes are accorded a special, morale-boosting status. After all, part of the country's fortunes still rest on the broad shoulders of the *macheteros*.

Cane-cutting and work in the mills used to be done by slaves. For planters, ship owners and traders, sugar yielded huge profits, as the Europeans couldn't get enough of the white gold. During the 18th century, drinking coffee became the height of fashion among the nobility and the middle classes, but the dark, bitter grains needed a sweetener – and the Caribbean crystal did the job perfectly.

MELTING AWAY

Sugar is Cuba's most important crop. Canes grow on every second square metre of agriculturally viable land with, in good years, two harvests ending in May. For decades, sugar was the main source of hard currency, but like crystals in a hot cup of coffee, this income has gradually melted away. Cuba's economic backbone is becoming weaker by the year, a situation made much worse by collapsing world prices and strong international competition.

In the factories, the machines are working again with the new Venezuelan oil imports. It is becoming more difficult to find *macheteros* – even though the State rewards them well, not just in wages, but also with fringe benefits such as extra food allowances and good living conditions. But

Filling the coffers
Until the early 1990s, Cubans did not have to pay taxes, but in 1994 the Government started taxing the income of the private entrepreneurs in order to cream off some of the large quantities of cash circulating in the black market.

Below: sugar press
Bottom: most of the heavy work is mechanised

they are working for worthless pesos – dollars would make all the difference to the men toiling in the fields.

COFFEE

During the 19th century, it was over a cup of coffee that businessmen negotiated, intellectuals argued, revolutionaries plotted, politicians schemed and Bohemians daydreamed. The relaxing aroma and the stimulating caffeine aided conversation. In Europe a whole new social world had grown up around this tempting beverage, and the café was a focal point for animated discussion. Some of these popular meeting places even used to be closed down as they were seen as breeding grounds for conspiracies and political intrigue. In Cuba, the coffee plantation owners were conspiring too, but they had only profit as a motive. Their objective was to maximise the production of coffee by minimising the cost of keeping slaves.

Cuba's first coffee beans, of African and Asian origin, were harvested in 1748. With the arrival of thousands of French colonists from Haiti at the end of the 18th century, when their slaves rose up against them, the cultivation of coffee in Cuba was given a massive boost, as the crop thrived in the red soil of the cooler uplands.

*Below: the finished product
Bottom: sugar plantation
house in the Valle de los
Ingenios, near the Sierra del
Escambray*

Bushes laden with the red fruit can be seen throughout the main coffee-growing areas of the Sierra de los Organos and Sierra del Rosario, near Pinar del Río, the Sierra Maestra and around the Sagua Baracoa mountains. Most of the *cafetales*, or coffee plantations, are in the Oriente, but the best coffee beans are grown on the slopes of the Sierra del Escambray near Trinidad. A constant temperature of about 21°C (70°F) and the quartz-rich soil provide the perfect conditions for the coffee bush.

CIGARS

Cuba is renowned throughout the world for the quality of its tobacco, and its cigars are the best in the world, with some 300 million being produced each year. During the 19th century, these brown, velvety cylinders became a symbol of wealth, intellect and individuality. Nevertheless, they'd been smoked for a long time before that – it just took a long time for the smoking habit to catch on with Europeans.

On his first trip to Cuba, Christopher Columbus observed that the Indians always had one of these unusual, glimmering brown objects hanging from their mouths. The conquistadors had only gold in mind, so when they breathed in the aromatic smoke for the first time, they are more

Below: Tobacco Museum, Pinar del Río
Bottom: landscape near Pinar del Río

likely to have collapsed with a coughing attack, not appreciating that *nicotiana tabacum* would one day be as valuable a raw material as the yellow metal they were seeking. Spanish explorer Hernán Cortés (1485–1547) regarded the custom as immoral and un-Christian.

But the brown sticks eventually found their way to Seville, and it was not long before the pleasures of inhaling the smoke from tobacco had spread to northern Europe. It was even smoked in churches, but the guardians of morality soon pronounced the habit as barbaric. Pope Urban VIII condemned the tobacco leaf as the devil's work. Tobacco became a source of controversy – and has remained one ever since.

The production of cigars in Havana did not start until the 18th century. In 1717, the Spanish Crown issued a decree granting itself sole manufacturing rights. The *factoría general* was established in Havana, with branches in Trinidad, Santiago de Cuba and Bayamo. But the Spaniards exploited its monopoly so assiduously and paid the tobacco farmers such a low figure for their crop that, in the end, it was more economical not to grow it at all. Production did not revive until 100 years later when the Spanish government finally abandoned its monopoly.

THE ART OF MAKING CIGARS

The region south of Pinar del Río, between San Luis, El Corojo and San Juan y Martínez offers the ideal climatic conditions for cultivating tobacco. Seeds are sown in September and October and the seedlings planted out in November. The plants have to be covered with cheesecloth in order to protect them from the strong sunlight, storms and insects. Unlike many other tropical plants, tobacco needs man's undivided attention and a Cuban saying goes: 'You cannot just plant tobacco, you have to marry it.'

The harvest starts three months later. First the leaves are removed and then left to dry in bundles in the *casas de tabaco*. The cured leaves are then packed in bales and sent off to Havana, where they

Favourite cigars
Sir Winston Churchill, rarely seen without a fat cigar, favoured Romeo y Julieta, whereas Castro preferred the Cohiba (invented after the Revolution). For Fidel Castro, the Havana cigar was just as important a part of his image as his straggly beard, but in 1990 when the Government ran a health campaign, he gave up smoking in public. His fellow Revolutionary Che Guevara, although an asthma sufferer, could not go without his *puro habano*.

Below: quality control
Bottom: a famous brand

are subjected to further treatment. Women do most of the work in the cigar factories. *Escoge-doras* examine the leaves and assess their quality and then the *rezagas* remove the central stalk.

Colour is important – it is possible to break down the leaves into 60 different shades. Other factors such as aroma and flammability are considered and then the leaves can be separated into inner and outer leaves. Every leaf has to be shaken and rolled smooth. *Rezagas* must prepare 1,000 leaves during a working day lasting eight hours, including one hour for lunch. Their monthly salary is in the region of 230 pesos (about US$8–9).

A cigar consists of three parts: the filler tobacco, depending on quality either rolled or cut, the binder leaf and the wrapper leaf, which must be flawless. Rolling a cigar properly is an art which requires great dexterity. The highly specialised *torcedores*, or cigar rollers, use three instruments: the *chaveta*, a sharp knife for cutting the leaves, a guillotine for making a smooth cut at the end to be lit, and a bowl containing a vegetable-based, neutral-tasting glue. The filler and binder are left in a press for 25 minutes before being wrapped in the best leaves, probably the hardest job of all. It is the quality of the wrapper leaf which determines the price. A *torcedor* can produce between 100 and 120 cigars per day.

Once completed, they are tied together in bundles and stored at a constant temperature. As proof of their authenticity, all the famous brands such as Cohiba, Romeo y Julieta, Montecristo, Partagás and H. Upmann are finished with a *vitola*, a band on which is written: *República de Cuba, hecho en Cuba.*

Below: tobacco drying
Bottom: Che, the revolutionary

THE REVOLUTIONARY YEARS

During his first presidency (1940–44), Fulgencio Batista acquired a reputation as a 'butcher', ruling by intimidation, torture and hunger. When he failed to be elected in 1952, he seized power and cancelled the elections. Students rebelled, and a 28-year-old lawyer named Fidel Castro Ruz accused the despot of breaching the Constitution. Castro's writ reached Batista's desk, but then it disappeared. As all legal methods of restoring the rule of law had failed, Castro argued, the only solution left was revolution. On the morning of 26 July 1953, Castro, leading 128 rebels disguised in uniforms similar to those of Batista's forces, attacked the Moncada Barracks in Santiago. However, the Government troops inside were alerted to the assault and fired back.

Most of the assailants were seized and many were tortured to death. Castro was brought before the courts, but he mounted a brilliant defence, accusing the Government of corruption. His words were received sympathetically by the dissatisfied population, including large sections of the middle classes, church leaders and army generals. 'Condemn me,' said Castro, 'but history will exonerate me' – '*La historia me absolverá*'. Found guilty, Castro and his brother Raúl were sent to the Modelo prison on Isla de la Juventud.

REBEL FORCES

In 1955, the two were banished to Mexico, where Fidel met the Argentinian revolutionary Che Guevara. There they got together a rebel force and on 2 December 1956, around 80 of them landed in Cuba in a small cabin cruiser, *Granma*. A

Fidel Castro

Fidel Castro Ruz was born on 13 August 1926 in Birán in northern Oriente. His father, who rose from Spanish infantryman to wealthy plantation owner, sent him to a Jesuit college, where he became known as a rebel. As a student and then as a lawyer, he was involved in the movement opposed to Batista.

Despite all the criticism levelled against the *Máximo Líder* (great leader), he is trusted by many of the Cuban people, as he was the first leader to really tackle social justice issues. He has renounced privileges and expressed solidarity with them.

Meanwhile, the bearded guerrilla has grown older. Today, when he addresses Western audiences to explain his foreign policy, he wears tailor-made suits instead of battle-dress. Times have changed.

Fidel sticks to his principles

Che Guevara

Ernesto 'Che' Guevara (born in 1928) has been depicted on posters throughout the world as a person who made a career out of revolution. This doctor from Argentina fought alongside Fidel Castro in the Sierra Maestra, then became Cuban Industry Minister and president of the National Bank of Cuba.

He was the principal ideologist of the post-Revolutionary era, responsible for the building of a socialist state and political education. His dream was the creation of a 'new human being', who put material interests to one side, who was selfless and who acted in solidarity with others. He earned a special place in the Cubans' hearts.

In 1965 differences arose between Che and Castro and he left to fight for the political revolution in the Congo. He died in pursuit of the socialist cause in Bolivia in 1967.

Keeping Cuba on the road, Varadero

skirmish with Batista's forces left just 22 alive, and they made for the Sierra Maestra. There they built up support for the Revolution and after a protracted struggle which ended with Guevara's attack on a troop train in Santa Clara on 29 December 1958, Batista fled.

POST-REVOLUTION

The two leaders immediately set about rebuilding a society along socialist lines. Castro dismantled the corrupt apparatus of state so thoroughly that hardly anything remained. After all the foreign, mainly American, possessions in Cuba had been confiscated, the US, Cuba's main trading partner, embarked on a policy of confrontation, reducing sugar imports by 95 percent and cutting off diplomatic relations in 1961.

Castro, who did not want to be tied up in an ideological straitjacket, looked in vain for allies. When it became clear that the country was slowly heading for economic catastrophe, he turned to the Soviet Union for succour. This led to the Cuban Crisis in 1962, when a Russian missile base was revealed on the island and a third world war was threatened. But under the protection of the superpower, Cuba enjoyed a period of prosperity, with living standards outstripping those of its neighbours in Central and South America.

GOVERNMENT

The Constitution of 1976 proclaimed Cuba as the 'Socialist Republic of Workers and Peasants' and the Partido Communista de Cuba (PCC), founded in 1966, became the official party of government. Fidel Castro has been Leader of the Government, Commander-in-Chief of the Armed Forces and General Secretary of the Communist Party of Cuba since 1959. The bearded ideologue wields all the power, aided by his charisma and his considerable rhetorical skills. In second rank is his brother and Defence Minister, Raúl. The remaining power lies with the 589-strong National Assembly, which elects the Council of State, also chaired by Fidel, and nominates the 44-strong Council of Ministers. Direct and secret elections have taken place since 1993. The official turn-out in 2003 was 97.6 percent.

Below: Fidel the orator
Bottom: Socialism or death

NO OPPOSITION

A Comité de Defensa de la Revolución (CDR) is assigned to every neighbourhood. As well as organising communal duties, such as blood donation or the supervision of children going to school, the CDR also monitors the population within its control. 'Defence of the Revolution' and keeping a sharp eye on those members of the community who are not involved with the CDR are closely related tasks. Women's groups, trade unions and youth organisations set the agenda politically. Fidel does not tolerate opposition.

The revisionist concepts of *glasnost* and *perestroika* have caused economic problems, but in political terms they have made little difference. Although the plight of the Cubans is desperate (2,500 people tried to leave in 2003), there is nevertheless a good degree of harmony between them and the Party. However, Cuba remains blacklisted by the American government, while the rest of the world tries to find ways to circumvent the embargo. Fear of Washington and the unknown poses a far greater threat than the fear of repression. Cuba, no longer protected, is learning that the price of independence is high.

HISTORICAL HIGHLIGHTS

circa **3500BC–AD1200** Arrival of the first Native American inhabitants, pre-ceramic hunter gatherer groups, who arrived in different waves after island-hopping from deltas such as the Mississippi and Orinoco. The Ciboney people appear with a similar, but more diverse, culture.

circa **AD1100** The Arawak Taínos settle on the island, living an agricultural existence. The Ciboney gradually become displaced and subservient to the Taínos.

1492 Christopher Columbus 'discovers' Cuba on 28 October, where there is already a native population of more than 100,000.

1508 Sebastián de Ocampo circumnavigates Cuba, establishing that it is indeed an island.

1512–15 Diego Velázquez takes over the island on behalf of the Spanish Crown, founding first Baracoa, on the east coast, followed by six other initial settlements around Cuba. Indigenous resistance to the Spanish crumbles when Cacique Hatuey, the great Indigenous chief, is burnt at the stake. The native population is eventually wiped out by the end of the 16th century.

1515 Santiago de Cuba becomes capital.

1522 The first slave ships arrive from Africa, with workers for the mines. Many of the Spanish settlers emigrate to other parts of the Empire, as no gold is found on the island.

1534 The first sugar mill opens.

1561 Spain establishes Havana as the assembly point for its silver fleet. Pirate attacks begin soon afterwards; the French pirate Jacques de Sores sacks Havana.

1662 The English Expedition commanded by Sir Christopher Myngs sacks Santiago.

1717 The tobacco trade is declared a Crown monopoly. Resistance from tobacco growers is crushed.

1762 Havana falls to a massive British invasion force. The port is opened up to international trade, breaking the earlier monopoly of the Spanish crown. The British encourage the slave trade to allow expansion of the plantation system.

1763 Havana returned to Spanish rule as Britain swaps Havana for Florida (Treaty of Paris).

1790s Sugar replaces tobacco as Cuba's most valuable export.

1795 About 30,000 French planters flee to Cuba from Haiti in advance of Toussaint l'Ouverture's slave rebellion. Cuba becomes the world's third-largest exporter of sugar.

1800s Beginnings of independence movements in Cuba. Simón Bolívar leads anti-colonial revolts across Latin America.

1868–78 In the First War of Independence, Cubans under Carlos Manuel de Céspedes fail in their struggle against Spanish rule.

1886 Abolition of slavery.

1895–8 Second War of Independence, at the beginning of which one of the leaders, José Martí, is killed.

1898 The US enters the colonial war. Spain cedes Cuba to the US. Cuba wins independence, but has to submit to a US military governor.

1901 A new constitution proposes the withdrawal of US troops, but the American government retains the unrestricted right to intervene.

1902 Cuba becomes a republic, but under US control. The US drops its right to intervene is dropped in 1934, but the naval base at Guantánamo remains in American hands.

1925 Gerardo Machado becomes president and runs the country as a military dictatorship.

1933 Sergeant Fulgencio Batista y Zaldívar stages a coup. He assumes the presidency in 1940 and rules until 1944.

1952 When Batista is not re-elected when trying to seek a second term, he seizes power by force.

1953 The attack on the Moncada Barracks under the leadership of Fidel Castro fails. After a two-year period in jail, Castro flees into exile in Mexico, where he meets Che Guevara.

1956 Castro and Guevara return to Cuba in the *Granma* and begin a guerrilla war based in the Sierra Maestra.

1959 The Revolution succeeds in ousting the hated Batista regime.

1959–65 Counter-Revolutionaries receive exit visas. About half a million wealthy Cubans leave the country.

1960 Thirty-six of the largest American companies are nationalised. The US government retaliates with trade sanctions.

1961 In April exiled Cubans, with the support of the CIA, attempt an invasion at the Bay of Pigs. In December Cuba becomes a Socialist Republic committed to Marxist-Leninist principles.

1962 The US imposes a total trade embargo. As a result, Cuba becomes dependent on the USSR. The world teeters on the brink of a world war until the Russians agree to withdraw their weapons.

1965 Che Guevara resigns from the Cuban government.

1968 Small businesses are nationalised and the establishment of a classless society becomes a government objective.

1980 Unrest becomes widespread among the population. More than 100,000 Cubans leave the country in what became known as the Mariel boatlift.

1991 The Soviet Union collapses and Russian aid comes to an end, heralding the start of chronic food and fuel shortages. Known as the 'Special Period'.

1993 The US dollar is legalised and a series of economic reforms initiated.

1994 The economic situation worsens and over 30,000 *balseros* ('raftsmen') leave Cuba for Miami on home-made rafts. US tightens immigration controls.

1996 The trade embargo intensifies.

1998 The Pope visits Cuba. The US agrees to the relaxation of some sanctions.

2000 The US agrees an amendment to the embargo exempting food and medicine.

2002 Hurricanes Isidore and Lili smash into Western Cuba, forcing mass evacuations and damaging the tobacco crop.

2003 Castro begins sixth term as president.

2004 Cuba censured by UN Human Rights Commission for its treatment of dissidents. The US tightens economic sanctions once more.

Map
on page
34

A safe haven
The Prohibition era from 1920 to 1933 was a turbulent period of American history, and kicked off Cuba's tourist industry. Millionaires, gamblers, mafia bosses and corrupt politicians sailed over from Florida to Havana in droves to drink as much alcohol as they wanted, spend freely, settle old scores and plot new ways of making money.

Below: staying in tune
Bottom: Old Havana

1: Havana

Havana – the very name has a magical ring to it. Known in Spanish as La Habana (the old lady), the city does indeed exude an elegant charm. With its fine colonial-style architecture, the city is addictive and stimulating, but it is also demanding and quite exhausting.

If you stroll along the wide boulevards and through the squares, Hollywood-inspired images of the Prohibition will immediately spring to mind. At night, when the meagre light from the bars is all that illuminates the streets, that erotic, but rather seedy atmosphere is almost palpable. It is no surprise that a famous menswear designer called his fragrance for men 'Havana'.

Sadly, the old lady has lost much of her glamour. It is true that decadence and decay contribute to the city's magical appeal, but Cuba's capital is in a sorry state, even if some of the buildings are undergoing a tourist-inspired renaissance. For much of the 1990s, cyclists had the streets almost to themselves. Cars are now returning and traffic jams are more common. The undisputed kings of the road remain the 1950s' vintage American Chevrolets, Cadillacs, Dodges, Buicks and motorcycles with sidecars. The owners of these ancient gas-guzzlers are experts in motor vehicle technology and improvisation. But when nothing can

be done about the engine or clutch that is in need of repair, then they sit inside and listen to Cuban salsa on the car radio.

However, standing before the tired remains of an earlier era are the heralds of capitalism. Now that the Government is prepared to tolerate a degree of economic liberalisation, the streets are beginning to stir again. And on the Malecón, seductively dressed girls await their next client.

OLD HAVANA

★★★**La Habana Vieja** (Old Havana), the historic, central quarter, contrasts sharply with the many new buildings that have sprung up in the suburbs of what is now a sprawling city of 2.5 million people. Many of the fine colonial-style houses in this 4 sq km (1½ sq mile) district have been renovated, funding was attracted in part by UNESCO designating Old Havana as a World Heritage Site in 1982. The sights on this walk can be viewed on foot within a day.

The best starting point is at the ★★ **Plaza de Armas ❶**. Dating from around 1519, when the city was founded, it is Havana's oldest square. During the colonial era, soldiers loyal to the Spanish king used it as a parade ground. Now Habaneros gather in the shade of the trees and stare at the passing tourists. A monument in the centre of the small park honours Carlos Manuel de Céspedes *(see page 85)* for his, albeit unsuccessful, struggle against Spanish colonial rule.

PALACIO DE LOS CAPITANES GENERALES

To the rear of the Cuban hero stands one of Havana's finest buildings, the ★★ **Palacio de los Capitanes Generales ❷**, which was built in 1776 as a residence for Cuba's captains general. They lived on the first floor while the ground floor was kept for slaves and horses. One of the rooms was furnished in readiness for a visit by the Spanish royal family, but they never actually came. In the 18th century, Governor Tacón ordered the cobbles in front of the palace to be replaced by

★

Star Attractions
• Old Havana
• Plaza de Armas
• Palacio de los Capitanes Generales

Preceding pages: Trinidad Below: Old Havana street Bottom: shades of past splendour

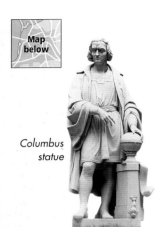

Columbus statue

wooden planks, as the clatter of horses' hoofs irritated him. After 1898 it became the residence of the US military governor, then that of the president, then the mayor and finally the museum director of the ★**Museo de la Ciudad** (daily 9am–6.30pm) which currently occupies the premises. It houses some fascinating exhibits, including works of art and colonial objects. If you would rather continue the walk, do not go without taking a look at the pretty patio with its columns and marble statue of Christopher Columbus.

Opposite the palace stands **El Templete** (Little Temple) and beside it a mighty ceiba tree, which is regarded as sacred. It was beneath a forerunner of this tropical tree that Havana is said to have been born and where the first Mass was

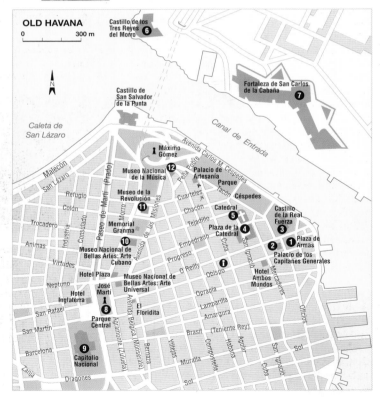

celebrated. On 16 November, the feast of Havana's patron saint San Cristóbal, many people queue up to walk around the tree three times and make a wish.

CASTILLO DE LA REAL FUERZA

Just a little further on is the ★ **Castillo de la Real Fuerza ❸**, which dates from 1538. It is not only the oldest fortress in Cuba but also one of the oldest in Latin America. Its walls, 6m (20ft) thick and 10m (33ft) high, were intended to protect the flourishing city from pirates. The round fortress tower is crowned by a small figure, known as La Giraldilla and now a symbol for Havana. Originally only a simple weather vane, it was replaced in 1632 by a bronze cast by Jerónimo Martínez Pinzón and represents Doña Inés de Bobadilla, the wife of the explorer Hernando de Soto. He is said to have insisted that for her own safety she remain within the fortress for as long as he was away. The first Giraldilla is kept in the Museo de la Ciudad and the emblem also appears on the Havana Club rum label. The Castillo, meanwhile, houses a small museum of Cuban ceramic art.

★ **Calle Obispo** starts to the west of the Plaza de Armas. This east-west shopping street is lined with cafés and restaurants and is one of the liveliest in Havana. Some of the houses have been faithfully restored, namely the Panadería San José and Drogería Johnson. About 200m (220yds) further on stands the beautifully renovated **Hotel Ambos Mundos**, where the novelist Ernest Hemingway used to stay.

HAVANA CATHEDRAL

At the heart of the Old Town lies the ★★★ **Plaza de la Catedral ❹**. Overlooked by a fine collection of buildings in Spanish colonial style, it is perhaps the most beautiful square in the city. It was here that the Cuban poet, Alejo Carpentier, declared Havana to be the 'City of Columns'. The huge ★ **Catedral ❺** in simple baroque dominates the square.

Star attraction
● **Plaza de la Catedral**

Hemingway's bed
In Room 511 of the Hotel Ambos Mundos in Calle Obispo, a made-up bed is kept just as it was when it was used by the American novelist Ernest Hemingway when he stayed in Cuba during the 1930s. The American novelist started writing his tale of the Spanish Civil War, *For Whom the Bell Tolls*, in this room, and you can visit it for US$2.

Below: Castillo de la Real Fuerza
Bottom: Hotel Ambos Mundos

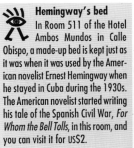

Map on page 34

Below: the Cathedral and a detail from a door
Bottom: inside La Bodeguita del Medio

A chapel stood on this site before the Jesuits started work on the present church in around 1750. However, the ambitious brethren were not to witness its consecration in 1788, as they were expelled from Cuba in 1767 in the name of the Spanish king. It is said that the bones of Christopher Columbus lay in the cathedral from when they were moved from Santo Domingo at the end of the 18th century until the end of the colonial war, whereupon they were shipped back to Spain.

To the right of the cathedral stands the beautiful, colonial 16th-century **Palacio de los Marqueses de Aguas Claras**, occupied by the well-run but pricey ★ **El Patio** café-restaurant which makes a good place for a break. On the left stand the 18th-century **Casa de Lombillo**, now headquarters of Dr. Eusebio Leal Spengler, the city historian, and the **Casa del Marqués de Arcos**, now an art gallery.

Bordering the south side of the cobbled square is the ★ **Casa Bayona** a.k.a. Casa Luis Chacón, a good example of a colonial mansion which houses an excellent little colonial museum, the **Museo de Arte Colonial** (San Ignacio 61; daily 9am–7pm) with some furnished rooms. Around the corner from the square, at Empedrado 207 is the ever popular **La Bodeguita del Medio**, one of Ernest Hemingway's favourite bars, where Cuba's national drink, the *mojito* was perfected.

A block northeast of the square towards the bay is the best artisans' market (Mercaderes y Chacón; Wednesday to Saturday 9am–6pm).

EL MORRO

The tour of Old Havana can end with an excursion to the other side of the Bahía de La Habana. This can be reached via the tunnel which starts near the Máximo Gómez monument. On a rocky mound, the ★★ **Castillo de los Tres Reyes del Morro** ❻, or simply El Morro, stands guard over the narrowest point of the harbour entrance. No other place in Havana offers such an all-embracing view of the capital's skyline. This fortress and the Castillo de San Salvador de la Punta opposite provided the Habaneros with a perfect vantage point, from where the progress of a potential enemy could be impeded with cross-fire. When in 1561 the harbour became the assembly point for the royal silver fleet before it returned to Spain, Havana rapidly became a prime target for pirates.

The solid El Morro bulwark, commissioned by King Philip II and built between 1589 and 1630, was for many years regarded as impregnable. But when in 1762 about 10,000 English soldiers closed in on the fortress with heavy guns from La Cabaña hill further to the east, El Morro quickly fell. One year later, Havana was returned to the Spanish in exchange for Florida. Soon after, the ★ **Fortaleza de San Carlos de la Cabaña** ❼, a fortress some 700m (750yds) in length, was built on the site of the battle. Beside the fortress walls is a bar with live music and dancing.

CENTRAL HAVANA

★ **Centro Habana** (Central Havana) is the name for the part of the city which lies to the west of the Old Town. When, during the 18th century, the expanding trading centre outgrew the immediate surroundings of the Plaza de Armas (see page 33), new building work started to the west towards the ★★ **Parque Central** ❽. Despite the proximity of the main thoroughfares, this large

Star Attractions
• Castillo de los Tres Reyes del Morro
• Parque Central

Out with a bang
Save a tour of the Fortaleza de San Carlos de la Cabaña for the evening to see the *Cañonazo de las Nueve* which takes place here daily at 9pm. In keeping with tradition, the cannon is fired by soldiers dressed in the colours of the Spanish colonial army, as a signal for the townsfolk to close the city gates.

El Morro

Map
on page
34

Independence fighter
José Martí is Cuba's greatest national hero with the standing of a saint. He is honoured with monuments, streets bearing his name and statues all over the country, one of which is in Parque Central. Born in Havana in 1853, his revolutionary verve came to the fore at the age of 25 when he helped found an anti-colonial newspaper against Spain. When only 17, his dissident views landed him in jail for several weeks. He was then deported to Spain until 1874, by which time he had become a journalist still championing the revolutionary cause.

Martí continued the struggle for independence, even during a second spell in exile in Mexico and the US. He returned to Cuba in April 1895 to lead the Second War of Independence but was killed a month later. Martí remains the father of Cuban nationalism and is revered as the pioneer of the Revolution.

The Gran Teatro

square, ringed by tall royal palms shading stone benches, is an oasis of calm. Grand hotels, such as the Inglaterra with its pillared portals and wrought-iron canopy (bar on the roof, often with live salsa music), and the yellow Plaza Hotel along with the 2,000-seat ★★ **Gran Teatro** in the Centro Gallego, give the square its part baroque, part neoclassical charm. A marble statue of the national revolutionary hero, José Martí, looks out over the park.

Diagonally opposite stands the vast ★ **Capitolio Nacional** ❾, a replica of Washington's Capitol, which was opened in 1929 under the hated President Machado. The building itself is equally unpopular, as it reminds the freedom-loving Cubans of the painful period of partial independence from the neighbouring super power and the puppet presidents the US kept in control. Since 1960 the Capitolio has been the seat of the Academy of Sciences; it is open to the public and worth a tour (8.30am–8pm, closed holidays).

CUBA'S OLDEST CIGAR FACTORY

To the west of the Capitolio is the ★★ **Real Fábrica de Tabacos Partagás**, the oldest cigar factory in Cuba still in use since its foundation in 1845. Here you can see cigar rollers at work (45-minute tours Monday to Saturday, every 15 minutes 9.30–11am and 12.30–3pm; no photographs) and buy from a wide selection of cigars in the shop.

The boulevard to the east of the Capitolio is officially called the ★ **Paseo de Martí** but is known as **El Prado**. Havana's grandest thoroughfare runs northwards to the sea, and some may detect traces of Madrid and Barcelona, or even Nice, along it, with tall trees and shaded stone benches down the centre and grand houses either side. The lions at the crossings are said to have been cast from the cannon that the English troops left behind in Havana.

Just east of the Prado, three blocks along towards the sea, you will find the ★★ **Museo**

Nacional de Bellas Artes 'Arte Cubano' (Tuesday to Saturday 10am–6pm, Sunday 10am–2pm) on Trocadero, behind the houses on the right, which exhibits a vast collection of Cuban paintings, with some works dating back to the colonial era. Of particular interest is the contemporary art on the second floor, plus the paintings of Wilfredo Lam *(see page 100)*.

Star Attractions
● **Gran Teatro**
● **Real Fábrica de Tabacos Partagás**
● **Museo Nacional de Bellas Artes**
● **Museo de la Revolución**

MUSEUM OF THE REVOLUTION

Continuing towards the sea, the former presidential palace on Refugio, which was once the residence of the hated dictator Fulgencio Batista, now accommodates the ★★ **Museo de la Revolución**  (Tuesday to Sunday 10am–5pm, Saturday to 6pm), where the stories behind the struggle for liberation and of the Revolution itself are fully documented. Visitors are presented with life-sized sculptures of the Revolutionaries in a faithfully reconstructed Sierra Maestra setting, and include Kalashnikovs, worn-out shoes, bloodstained shirts and even the same plates that the *guerrilleros* ate from. Other relics include an array of surgical instruments with which Che Guevara treated his wounded men.

Below: heroes of the Sierra Maestra in the Museo de la Revolución
Bottom: a bullet-riddled van

One of the prized exhibits is the **Memorial Granma** in the garden behind the museum. The motor yacht *Granma* that carried Fidel Castro

**Maps
on pages
34 and 42**

Best ice cream
Only a stone's throw away from the Hotel Nacional on La Rampa is the ★★ **Coppelia**, Havana's most famous ice cream parlour, which came to the attention of European film-goers after the release in 1994 of *Fresa y Chocolate* (Strawberry and Chocolate). Here you can sample the best ice cream in Havana without queuing – but only if you pay in dollars.

*Below: Malecón facades
Bottom: bathers out along
the Malecón*

from Mexico to Cuba in 1956 is now kept in a glass structure. It is difficult to imagine that it was this tiny vessel, loaded with 84 guerrilla fighters, plus supplies and weapons, that triggered the Revolution *(see pages 24–6)*. Close by is a tractor converted into a tank and a bullet-riddled delivery van. There is a changing of the guard ceremony here every afternoon at 3pm.

NATIONAL MUSEUM OF MUSIC

Nearer the sea is the **Museo Nacional de la Música** ⑫ (Cárcel 1 e/ Habana y Aguiar; Monday to Saturday 10am–5.30pm, closed Sunday) founded by the anthropologist, Fernando Ortíz. On view is the background to Cuba's musical history – from yellowing scores, strange instruments and African drums to a collection of old record players which visitors are invited to use.

At the end of El Prado, the famous ★ **Malecón** promenade, once part of the town's fortifications, extends along the seafront for over 3km (2 miles) from Old Havana as far as the **Miramar** diplomatic quarter. Before the Revolution, the wives of American millionaires frequented the fashionable jewellery shops here. Now, the area is rather run down, but it is at least brightened up at carnival time by a colourful procession led by dancers and drummers.

VEDADO (NEW HAVANA)

Just how much Havana has expanded is clear from the length of the Malecón. To walk from Centro Habana to the **Vedado** business and hotel quarter takes about 45 minutes, so it is wise to take a taxi.

Calle 23 or **La Rampa** is Havana's main artery. Every large company and airline has an address either on La Rampa or in one of the side streets. During the 1930s such infamous *mafiosi* as Lucky Luciano and Meyer-Lansky held wild parties at the ★ **Hotel Nacional** here *(see page 123)*. Other guests have included Winston Churchill and Charles de Gaulle, and fabled film stars Errol Flynn, Buster Keaton, Ava Gardner and Marlon

Brando have all sunned themselves by the hotel's swimming pool. The actor Johnny Weissmuller, famous for his big-screen portrayal of Tarzan, is said to have flung himself from his first floor room into the pool below.

HAVANA UNIVERSITY

Just off La Rampa on Vedado hill stands the **Universidad de La Habana**, which was founded by Dominican monks. The entrance hall takes the form of a vast, steep staircase, and during the Machado and Batista dictatorships, the steps were frequently the scene of fierce student protests; a monument to the student leader, Julio Antonio Mella, stands here. This dedicated fighter against imperialism and social injustice was murdered in 1929 by agents of the 'Mussolini of the Tropics', as Mella described Machado.

At Calle San Lazaro No. 661, to the northeast of the campus, stands the **Casa de la Trova**. Many Cuban towns have such cultural centres used by local people as venues for concerts, exhibitions, poetry readings and evening entertainment.

Below: Che looks on,
Plaza de la Revolución
Bottom: José Martí monument,
Plaza de la Revolución

PLAZA DE LA REVOLUCION

It is worth taking a detour into the newer part of Havana in the south to see the ★★ **Plaza de la**

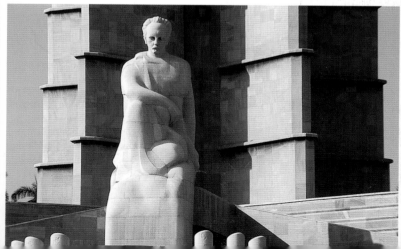

Maps
on pages
42 and 44

Revolución ⑬, between Avenida Carlos M. de Céspedes and Rancho Boyeros. A giant monument to José Martí stands in the centre and you can now take a lift to the top. The most striking building overlooking the square is the Ministry of the Interior building, which bears an illuminated mural of Che. When Fidel wishes to speak to the nation, it is here that the crowds gather and as many as 1 million people have attended rallies in the square.

It is only a 10-minute walk to the **★★ Cementerio del Colón ⑭** (Zapata y Calle 12; daily 9am–5pm). With its vast gateway, elaborate gravestones and marble mausoleums, this central cemetery, laid out in 1871, ranks among the finest graveyards in the world. United in death, sugar barons and revolutionaries lie side by side.

EXCURSIONS

The journey from the city centre southeastwards to the **★ Museo Casa Ernest Hemingway** (San Francisco de Paula; 9am–4.30pm, closed Tuesday and in heavy rain; tel: 07-910809), on the outskirts of the city, will take about 40 minutes by car. Ernest Hemingway moved to Finca Vigía because his third wife, Martha Gellhorn, had had enough of staying in hotels, but he missed his favourite bars in the city, the Bodeguita del Medio and the Floridita.

The Cubans' favourite *Yanqui* lived here from 1939 until he left Cuba in 1960 to undergo treatment for cancer. He donated both his Nobel Prize medal and his estate to the Cuban people. Everything in the house is practically as he left it, so visitors are not allowed to enter the rooms, but may only view them through the open windows. Bullfighting posters and hunting trophies from Africa hang on the wall, and some 9,000 books and newspapers are stacked in tall piles. A pair of his shoes is still airing beneath the window.

Hemingway wrote in his bedroom, sitting barefoot and striking the keys on his typewriter so hard that he called it his Royal Machine Gun. Photographs of his three children adorn the walls alongside guns and badges. His Mannlicher carbine is also on display: much to their consternation, with the gun unloaded, he used to show his wife and friends how he would one day commit suicide. In the Spanish dining room the table is set for three people: himself, his wife and the next guest. Many famous Hollywood names used to visit the writer here including Gary Cooper, Errol Flynn, Ingrid Bergman, Humphrey Bogart, Ava Gardner and Spencer Tracy; France's celebrated literary couple, Jean-Paul Sartre and Simone de Beauvoir, were also on the guest list.

GUANABACOA

Also southeast of Havana is the recently renovated **Museo Histórico de Guanabacoa** (Martí 108 e/San Antonio y Versalles; Monday, Wednesday–Saturday 10.30am–6pm, Sunday 9am–1pm), an ethnological museum which devotes its rooms mainly to the Regla de Ocha religious sect, usually known as Santería *(see page 103)*, and other Afro-Cuban religions such as Palo de Monte and the secret Abakuá group. Items on display include the sacred objects used by priests during their

Star Attraction
● **Cementerio del Colón**

Below: Ernest Hemingway – at home in Cuba
Bottom: Cojímar kids

Map below

Fishermen of Cojímar

ceremonies. However, it's all in Spanish so some knowledge of the language would be useful.

COJÍMAR

The Hemingway theme continues to the east of Havana in the fishing village of **Cojímar**, home of Gregorio Fuentes, a fisherman who continued to regale visitors with tales of his hero Hemingway until his death in 2002 at the age of 104. He was one of the few Cubans who was able to recall the writer personally until the end of the century, and attained almost as much notoriety as his former boss. Gregorio used to accompany him on fishing trips as skipper of the *Pilar*. Although he claimed not to be the same man who spent 84 days drifting with the Gulf Stream without catching a single fish and who is the subject of *The Old Man and The Sea*, he did not dispute that it was in Cojímar that Hemingway found the inspiration for the novel that won him the Pulitzer Prize in 1953 and the Nobel Prize in 1954.

MARINA HEMINGWAY

To the west of Havana lies the **Marina Hemingway** complex (Calle 48, Santa Fe Playa), with restaurants, hotels, boating and other facilities. Over the years, the salty air has nibbled away at the fabric of the buildings, and they are badly in

HAVANA DISTRICTS
0   3 km
EL Morro · Fortaleza de San Carlos de la Cabaña · COJÍMAR
VEDADO
CENTRO HABANA
LA HABANA VIEJA
Bahía de La Habana
MIRAMAR
Marina Hemingway
KOHLY · NUEVO VEDADO · CERRO
GUITERAS
BUENAVISTA · ALDECOA
REGLA
PALATINO · LUYANO
GUANABACOA · Museo Hist. de Guanabacoa
SANTA CATALINA · LA VIBORA
LA PAZ
POGOLOTTI · Airport
San Francisco de Paula
N

need of renovation. There's not a lot to see or do here and, in spite of the name, the place has no real connection with Hemingway. The famous annual marlin fishing tournament held in Hemingway's honour actually takes place out of **Tarará** marina to the east of the city and is held in May or June, when some of the biggest marlin run.

Star Attraction
● Playas del Este

BEACHES

In the absence of palm trees and fine sand, Miramar and La Playa, the beaches to the west of Havana, are not in the same league as those in the eastern ★★ **Playas del Este** district. Situated about 20km (12 miles) from the city centre, these seven sandy beaches beside the crystal blue Atlantic compare favourably with the beaches of Varadero *(see pages 50–2)*. And they can easily be reached on the motorway from Havana. On the outskirts of the city are the mass-produced flats that Castro built to overcome the dire housing shortage he inherited. One of every two homes in Cuba has been built since 1959 and, today, the slums that characterise so many Latin American countries have been more or less eradicated.

The **Blue Belt** – blue sky, blue water and white sandy shores – begins soon after. This is a sunshine paradise that the Cuban and American bourgeoisie discovered in the 1950s. They built luxurious residences and cordoned off sections of the beach for themselves. The best of the seven beaches are **Bacuranao**, **El Mégano**, **Boca Ciega** and **Guanabo**, with wooden bungalows dating from the 1920s and 1930s; but ★ **Santa María del Mar** is the most popular with the most hotels. Here you can relax on a wide strip of sand beside lagoons or under coconut palms and reach the offshore coral reefs in minutes. Jibacoa and Tropico, the two other beaches, are separated by rocks.

Near the fishing village of **Santa Cruz del Norte** is Cuba's largest rum distillery where the famous Habana Club brand is produced, and just inland is the **Central Camilo Cienfuegos** sugar mill founded by the American Hershey Chocolate Company in 1917.

Below: sink or swim
Bottom: beach boy

Map
on pages
48–9

Below: coastal contrasts
Bottom: bridge across
the Yumurí

2: Along the Coast to Varadero

Havana – Matanzas – Varadero (140km/87 miles)

When you see the Caribbean dream depicted in the travel brochures – crystal-clear water, a bright blue sky, miles and miles of white, fine-grained sand – then that is Varadero. The images are perfect, perhaps a little corny, and many people may even have an uneasy feeling that something is not quite right, maybe it is just another piece of clever photography. But you can rest assured. These pictures have not been 'doctored', but are an accurate reflection of reality. The water is, in fact, azure blue and, when you lie on the wave-washed sand for the first time, you will surely notice how fine and soft it is. There might, however, be fewer palm trees than you imagined.

Varadero on the Hicacos Peninsula is Cuba's tourist mecca. Set between lagoons, coral beaches and mangrove forests it is, however, a world from which the ordinary Cuban is excluded. As the island's socialist managers have had to disregard their ideological principles in the interests of survival, Varadero has developed into a divided town.

It only takes a few hours to reach the resort of Varadero from Havana. Even if you stop off in Matanzas, a town whose prosperity has been built on sugar and tobacco.

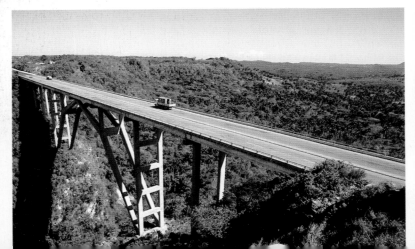

YUMURI VALLEY

After about 95km (59 miles), you reach the **Puente de Bacunayagua**. The view from the bridge across the 112-m/370-feet deep ★★ **Yumurí Valley** takes in the lush palm groves, the distant mountains, the turkey vultures circling above them and the white and blue coastline. Having gradually cut its way through the limestone gorge, the River Yumurí eventually opens out into the Atlantic.

Soon after the bridge, you will be able to make out the sheltered **Bahía de Matanzas** and the rather less attractive outline of industrial Matanzas (100km/60 miles).

MATANZAS

Despite the many factories, ★★ **Matanzas** (pop. 120,000) is one of the finest cities in Cuba. This port, founded at the end of the 17th century, enjoyed an enormous boost first from exporting tobacco and then sugar. It was also the port of arrival for many of the African slaves and, not surprisingly, uprisings occurred here frequently. And yet the pesos poured in, bestowing untold riches on many of its inhabitants. It quickly assumed a leading role in economic and cultural matters, with many new ideas emerging from the think tanks that were spawned by many of the city's intellectuals.

There is still plenty of evidence of this period of prosperity: in the heart of the old town, with the narrow alleys in chequerboard style, stand many fine, partially restored town houses with columns and wrought-iron doors, dating from the heyday of the sugar planters. As in every Spanish colonial town, the centre has grown up around a *plaza*. Here it is called the **Parque de la Libertad**, with State (the *Ayuntamiento* or Town Hall) and Church greeting each other in harmony.

The **Catedral San Carlos** is a large neo-classical structure dating from 1878. There was also a casino here once, but the puritanical Revolutionaries replaced it with a library.

Star attractions
- Yumurí Valley
- Matanzas

Magnificent *mirador*
At the western end of the impressive Puente de Bacunayagua, which spans the 112m (370ft) deep river gorge, there is a viewpoint for the classic photo opportunity of the Yumurí Valley, complete with the obligatory souvenir stalls and a small restaurant and café.

Cathedral San Carlos in Matanzas

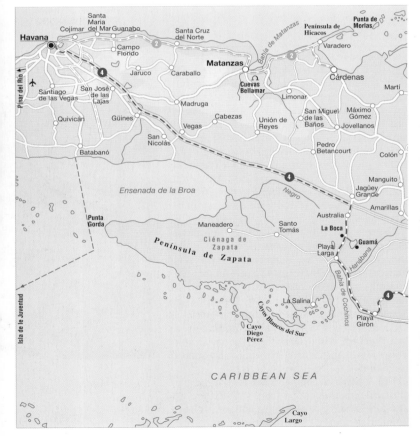

Pharmaceutical Museum

The main attraction beside the square is the ★**Museo Botica Farmacéutico Francesa Dr E. Triolet** (Monday to Saturday 10am–6pm, Sunday 10am–2pm) a pharmaceutical museum in an old chemist's shop. It is easy to imagine the elderly Dr Triolet standing behind the cedarwood shelving preparing a potion of herbs and powders to his own special recipe. In fact, the shop was in use for the sale of pills and ointments until 1964. Since it opened in 1882, the doctor had collected a huge stock of small bottles and porcelain jars from Bohemia and France. Also on display are distilling flasks, mortars, scales, surgical equipment and a wood-burning brick oven.

Just to the east of the square lies the imposing ★ **Teatro Sauto** (Plaza de la Vigía), which dates from 1862 and is noted for its fine acoustics. With seats for 750 people, the classical musical and theatrical evenings held here are clearly aimed at a well-educated public. By putting up the funds for this ornate, neoclassical theatre, the patron, named Sauto, created a lasting memorial to himself.

About 3km (2 miles) southeast of Matanzas, slaves working in a quarry in 1861 discovered the ★★ **Cuevas de Bellamar**, which is the largest

Star Attraction
● **Cuevas de Bellamar**

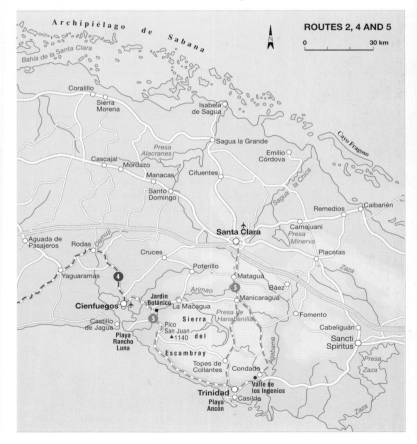

Archipiélago de Sabana

Bahía de la Santa Clara

ROUTES 2, 4 AND 5

0   30 km

Coralillo

Sierra Morena

Isabela de Sagua

Sagua la Grande

Cayo Fragoso

Presa Alacranes

Cascajal

Mordazo

Emilio Córdova

Manacas

Cifuentes

Santo Domingo

Sagua la Chica

Remedios

Caibarién

Aguada de Pasajeros

Rodas

Cruces

Santa Clara

Camajuaní

Presa Minerva

Placetas

Damují

Poterillo

Yaguaramas

④

Matagua

Arimao

⑤

Báez

Cienfuegos

Jardín Botánico

La Macagua

Manicaragua

Fomento

Castillo de Jagua

⑤

Sierra

Pico San Juan
▲1140

Presa de Hanabanilla

Cabeliguán

Playa Rancho Luna

del

Sancti Spíritus

Escambray

Agabama

Presa Zaza

Topes de Collantes

Condado

Trinidad

Valle de los Ingenios

Playa Ancón

Casilda

Zaza

Map on pages 48–9

Below: encounters on the beach
Bottom: the marina at Varadero

accessible cave complex in Cuba. The darkness underground was regarded as Satan's lair for at least 100 years, but pressure from explorers to investigate eventually prevailed. In order to open up the passages, which are almost 2km (1¼ miles) in length, thousands of tons of rock had to be removed and it took three weeks to pump out all the water. A fascinating world of crystalline stone such as the 'Columbus Mantle', a crystal formation like a folded curtain over 12m (40ft) high, came to light. The largest cave, the 'Gothic Chamber', is 80m (260ft) long and 25m (82ft) wide.

A highway, the Via Blanca, runs 32km (20 miles) eastwards from the caves beside a partly rocky, partly sandy coastline – dotted with oil rigs flying the Cuban and Canadian flags to demonstrate their joint venture – as far as the Laguna de Paso Malo bridge, which connects the 20-km (12-mile) Hicacos Peninsula with the mainland.

VARADERO

Ahead lies Cuba's largest and most exclusive holiday resort, ★★ **Varadero** (140km/87 miles). The chain of hotels is now as long as the beach itself which stretches along the peninsula's entire Atlantic coastline. The countless cranes speak for themselves, but you will have to look hard for anything of interest in the town of Varadero itself (pop.

10,000), at the base of the peninsula. A few plain, wooden villas, originally belonging to wealthy planters, who made tourism fashionable towards the end of the 19th century, are of architectural note. One or two other attractive houses date from the turn of the 20th century, when this holiday playground started to attract North American millionaires. After the Revolution, their villas were taken over by the State for hotels or housing.

You can get a small taste of the Cuban lifestyle in Varadero along the Bahía de Cárdenas coast, but you'll still feel a million miles from the 'real' Cuba. That said, it becomes a quiet and relaxing spot around here in the evenings, as the few Cubans who do live here sit out on their verandahs in their rocking chairs and seesaw the hours away. Armed with only a few words of Spanish, it is easy to make contact with them.

In the **Parque Retiro Josone,** to the north of the town, it is not just extended Cuban families who get together here at weekends, but also artists displaying their paintings and souvenir sellers hawking their home-made products to tourists. A variety of restaurants and bars cater for those in need of refreshment, and in the evenings Afro-Cuban shows on the open-air stage (followed by a disco) help to prolong the lively atmosphere.

VILLA LAS AMERICAS

Towards the western tip of the peninsula, on a hill directly above the cliffs, lies the **Mansión Xanadú**, which once belonged to the French-born multi-millionaire industrialist, Alfred Irénée Du Pont de Nemours. His palatial summer residence is open to visitors, but the wine cellars and organ can be seen only by appointment – plus a certain amount of luck.

It is said that in 1929 when Du Pont built his four-storey house, known as Xanadu, it cost US$1.3 million, and that the furniture alone cost US$200,000. Bricklayers were brought over from Italy and told to mix goat's milk into the cement to give it a gentler sheen. Du Pont made access to the upper floors easier by installing a lift. On the

Star Attraction
● Varadero

In the dry
For anyone who is not keen on snorkels and diving equipment, an underwater excursion on the Varasub is the ideal alternative. There is no need to change into a wetsuit to see through a glass floor the shoals of fish darting around the coral reefs. The boat departs six times a day from the Punta Blanca in the Laguna de Paso Malo. For more details, contact Tour & Travel, Avenida Playa 3606 e/ Calle 36 y Calle 37, tel: 045-63713.

Below: fun in the sun

Map
on pages
48–9

Land speculator

Alfred Irénée Du Pont, who made his fortune in World War I by selling dynamite, and later cigarette lighters, fountain pens and nylons, bought up practically the whole of the Hicacos Peninsula north of Varadero in 1926. He paid only a paltry 4 centavos for each square metre and, after improving the infra-structure, he sold it in parcels of land to wealthy American industrialists and politicians at 120 pesos per square metre. Shielded from the eyes of the rest of the world, Cuba's corrupt politicians and dictators were at liberty to negotiate their shady deals with foreign businessmen in peace.

Arriving in style at Mansión Xanadú

ground floor, there's a large dining room, several sitting rooms, a tea room, a library and an office. The Italian marble floors are original, as are the mahogany ceiling and sweeping banister.

One of the bedrooms on the first floor was reserved for his Polish lover, and from his own bedroom, he could enjoy a spectacular view out to sea. The bathrooms were fitted out with armchairs so that his four daughters could apply their make-up in comfort. One of them loved playing the organ, so her father had a huge one built in 1932 at a cost of US$110,000. When the wind blew from the south, her playing could be heard for miles around.

He kept seven cars in the garage, bred iguanas as a hobby, played golf and ran a sisal factory in Cárdenas. Altogether, he employed 76 people on his estate – servants, guards, gardeners and animal keepers. It is also said that Du Pont kept a private army of guards for his own personal protection around the estate.

Soon after the Revolution, Du Pont's estate was nationalised. In February 1959, the Revolutionaries announced that all the beaches were public property. Du Pont was 80 when, shortly before his death in 1963, he eventually left the country. His house, which now bears the name Mansión Xanadú, has been converted into a hotel and also contains an expensive French restaurant (daily 7am–11.30pm) and a top-floor bar.

LIMESTONE CAVES

The **Cueva de Ambrosio**, about 5km (3 miles) further along the peninsula, was discovered in 1961. This small cave, about 8.5m (28ft) above sea level, found among limestone caves in the Parque Natural de Varadero, was immediately searched by archaeologists for prehistoric paintings. About 40 or so drawings were found – some were the well-preserved centuries-old work of native Amerindians, others depicted African figures and are believed to have been drawn by black slaves, possibly escapees who came here to hide and who performed ritual ceremonies.

3: The Extreme West

Havana – Soroa – Pinar del Río – Valle de Viñales (202km/125 miles)

Map on pages 54

The province of Pinar del Río has very little to offer in the way of historical or cultural sights, in fact the town of the same name is sometimes described as 'Cuba's Cinderella'. In scenic terms, however, the region has a unique beauty. No part of the country has so many palm trees, mainly royal palms and *barrigonas* or big belly palms – the latter only grow in the far west of the island.

The fertile earth is copper coloured, and extensive areas of green forests and mountains alternate with plantations. The brown dots of the *bohíos*, the palm-covered peasant huts, or of the sheds where tobacco leaves are dried, proliferate. Black turkey vultures circle elegantly in the sky – on closer inspection, their bare and wrinkly red heads are frighteningly ugly. A bizarre geological phenomenon – overgrown *mogotes* or 'haystack' hills – can be seen in the Valle de Viñales.

Below: old timers in Pinar del Río
Bottom: shower time at Soroa

SOROA

If you are coming from Havana on the *autopista*, you will first pass the Sierra del Rosario (a UNESCO Biosphere Reserve), which is the more easterly of the two medium-range mountain

Map
on page
54

Las Terrazas

About 10km (7 miles) to the east of Soroa, in the heart of the forest, is the eco-resort of Las Terrazas, which started life in 1967 as an artists' colony. Artists still live in a shabby complex, built among the trees on the terraced land running down to a lake, selling their crafts and art. Now an eco-centre has been added, providing knowledgeable guides who can show you the abundant flora and birdlife around the forest trails. Visitors can stay in the Hotel La Moka *(see page 124)*, a modern hotel which blends well with the surroundings.

chains in the province. In 1943, a botanical garden was laid out near the tiny village of ★★ **Soroa** (85km/53 miles), which lies 7km (4 miles) north of the motorway. About 25,000 different species occupy the 35,000 sq-m (40,000 sq-yd) site. As well as magnolias, philodendron, hibiscus shrubs, palms and ferns from all parts of the globe, there is an ★ **Orquideario**, of which every inhabitant of Soroa is very proud. Some 700 different orchid species thrive here, about 250 of which are native to Cuba. A small waterfall flows into the Baño de San Juan thermal spring, and if you take a swimming costume you can have an exhilarating shower under it. The sulphurous water is said to have healing powers.

PINAR DEL RIO

The provincial capital of **Pinar del Río** (175km/108 miles), at the foot of the Sierra de los Organos, is a lively town with a population of 140,000. Before it was founded in 1571, it was, as its name suggests, surrounded by pine forests, but these were razed for tobacco fields. One of the most notable public buildings is the neoclassical ★ **Teatro Milanés** built in the 19th century by the town's tobacco-farming *bourgeoisie*, whose wealth came from tobacco.

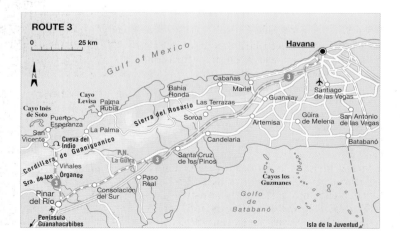

ROUTE 3

0   25 km

N

Gulf of Mexico

Havana

Cabañas
Bahía Honda
Mariel
Guanajay
Santiago de las Vegas
Cayo Levisa
Palma Rubia
Las Terrazas
Cayo Inés de Soto
Puerto Esperanza
Soroa
Artemisa
Güira de Melena
San Antonio de las Vegas
San Vicente
La Palma
Cueva del Indio
Sierra del Rosario
Candelaria
Batabanó
Cordillera de Guaniguanico
R.N. La Güira
Santa Cruz de los Pinos
Viñales
Sra. de los Órganos
Paso Real
Cayos los Guzmanes
Pinar del Río
Consolación del Sur
Golfo de Batabanó
Península Guanahacabibes
Isla de la Juventud

The first tobacco factory was established here in 1760. At the ★**Fábrica de Tabacos Francisco Donatién** near the Plaza de la Independencia, you can see the workers here roll leaves of *nicotiana tabacum* into cigars, and buy a box to take home. Non-smokers may prefer the local liqueur called *Guayabita*, made from the small guayabita fruit, endemic to the region.

Star Attractions
● **Soroa**
● **Fábrica de Tabacos Francisco Donatién**
● **Valle de Viñales**

VALLE DE VINALES

Leaving Pinar del Río on the northbound road to Viñales, you enter the remarkable world of the Sierra de los Organos mountains. Emerging out of the flat ★★★ **Valle de Viñales** are a series of limestone rocks about 400m (1,300ft) high. The origins of these *mogotes*, or 'elephants' backs' as they are known locally, go back 160 million years.

Research has revealed that the hills are the result of tropical erosion caused by a network of underground streams eating away at the limestone bedrock and forming caverns. These eventually collapsed, leaving behind the eroded remains we see today. When the mists rise, the valley basks in an almost magical power that has a soothing effect. For the best view of the *mogotes*, book into the friendly **Los Jazmines** hotel *(see page 125)*.

MURAL OF PREHISTORY

Shortly before you reach the little town of Viñales, branch off to the left and, a few miles further on in the Valle de las Dos Hermanas, you will come across an unusual, if rather kitsch, work of art known as the **Mural de la Prehistoria**.

Prehistoric men and beasts have been drawn on the wall in coloured chalks as a reminder of the long life of the *mogotes*. The idea for the mural came from a scientist, Nuñez Jiménez. Leovigildo González Morillo, a mural specialist and a student of Mexican artist Diego Rivera (1886–1957), was flown in to complete the 120-m (400-ft) high by 180-m (590-ft) wide painting in 1964. In the restaurant here, guests can sit beneath the *bohío*

Below: working the fields
Middle: Sierra de los Organos
Bottom: Mural de la Prehistoria

Map
on page
54

Fat Mary
At the extreme western end of Cuba, where the two *cabos*, San Antonio and Corrientes, form the Bahía de Corrientes, lies the magnificent 8-km (5-mile) long beach known as María La Gorda or 'Fat Mary'. This remote spot is frequented by ecotourists and diving enthusiasts looking for peace and quiet. They normally stay in the appealing María La Gorda Villa hotel *(see page 125)*. Nearby is a new jetty where an international scuba centre is based, giving access to more than 50 diving sites.

Cueva del Indio

roof and sample the delicious house speciality, *cerdo asado y ahumado* (roast suckling pig).

THE INDIAN CAVE

Of the many caves in the Valle de Viñales, the **Cueva del Indio** (daily 9am–5pm), 8km (5 miles) north of Viñales, receives most visitors. An underground river wore away at the rock for millions of years to form this 4-km (2½-mile) long cavern. Probably used by the Indians as a hiding place when the Spanish were scouring the Caribbean islands for gold, it was not rediscovered until 1920. It needs a degree of imagination to make the link between the names given to the rock formations, such as the Three Ships of Columbus, the Sea-horse, the Iguana and the Giant Snake. Part of the tour involves a 10-minute ride along the underground river, the Río San Vicente, on a noisy and foul-smelling motorboat.

BEACHES

★★ **Cayo Levisa**, a small coral cay to the north of Pinar del Río, still carries an exclusive tag. To get there, you have to take the ferry from Palma Rubia (25-minute trip, boat leaves at 10am and 6pm, returns from Cayo Levisa 9am and 5pm). The beautiful, sandy beach on the island *(see picture on page 6)* will be shared with the few dozen other hotel guests and daytrippers, and the small diving centre there does not even have the facilities to replenish oxygen tanks. Overnight accommodation is available in the simple, but attractive **Villa Cayo Levisa** bungalow complex *(see page 125)*, which has a restaurant and a bar, but reserve in advance. Cayo Levisa is a lovely destination, with good opportunities for snorkelling and diving.

Most tourists who visit this end of Cuba turn back at Pinar del Río. But to reach the westernmost point on the **Guanahacabibes Peninsula**, you will have to drive for another 110km (68 miles) through rather monotonous countryside, although the end of the route goes through a national park.

4: The South Coast

Havana – Zapata Peninsula – Bay of Pigs – Guamá – Cienfuegos (274km/170 miles)

Map on page 48–9

Wherever you look, there are open fields with pineapple plants, orange trees and, of course, sugar cane. In between are huge expanses of grassland, where herds of cattle graze. The strip of land through Matanzas Province from Havana to Cienfuegos resembles one huge, endless plantation. This is the centre of the sugar industry. During the harvest between November and May, to both right and left of the road, huge cane-cutting machines and *macheteros* can be seen performing their back-breaking work chopping down the tall canes.

Star Attraction
● Cayo Levisa

*Below: Indian sculpture
at Guamá
Bottom: boat trip through
the swamps*

THE ZAPATA PENINSULA

On the other hand, the Zapata Peninsula is deserted. You can take a boat ride through mangrove swamps *(ciénaga)* with only cheeps, chirrups and crackles echoing through the swampy thicket. It is rare now to encounter a crocodile, but there are countless different species of fish and birds, not to mention huge swarms of voracious mosquitoes.

In the picturesque natural harbour of Jagua Bay, the small provincial capital of Cienfuegos still reveals some of its French heritage.

Map on pages 48–9

Zapata Mangrove Swamps

On the southbound *autopista* from Havana, you will overtake pedestrians, cyclists, horse and ox carts, sometimes even a truck, but not too many other cars. Progress is fast and you could easily cover the route in one day, but if you want to stay at places you will need longer.

The sugar cane fields end where the road branches off to the ★★ **Ciénaga de Zapata National Park** (Parque Nacional Ciénaga de Zapata) on the Zapata Peninsula south of Jagüey Grande (122km/75 miles). The nature reserve extends over 285,000 hectares (70,000 acres) of mangrove swamps, dry and seasonally-flooded woodland and expanses of sawgrass. Mangroves are tropical trees that love coastal regions, river mouths and muddy bays. They put out a network of strong roots reinforcing the land against erosion.

Some 87 percent of all the bird species on Cuba live in the Ciénaga. With luck and lots of patience, the experienced birdwatcher armed with binoculars ought to be able to spot a rare *zunzuncito*, the smallest bird in the world at only 63mm (2½in).

Crocodiles used to be plentiful in this area, but most of them have been wiped out by hunters. Compensating for this decline in numbers is the world's second-largest ★ **crocodile farm** (daily 8am–6pm) in the tourist centre of **La Boca**, about

Below: crocodile farmer
Bottom: holiday huts at Guamá

15km (8 miles) after the motorway turn-off. The 8,000 or so crocodiles (80–90 percent get eaten in the tourist restaurant here) in the circular enclosures not only keep the species alive, but also ensure that elegant boutiques can continue to supply genuine crocodile skin handbags to wealthy women.

In the **Rancho** restaurant at La Boca, the delicious, roasted flesh of the crocodile is served up to diners – there are few other places where you can sample this meat, so you might wish to take the opportunity if you can.

GUAMA HOLIDAY VILLAGE

La Boca is also the starting point for 30-minute boat trips through sawgrass and reeds to **Guamá**, an Indian-style holiday village *(see page 125)* featured on many tour itineraries. At the end of the canal lies the **Laguna del Tesoro** (Treasure Lake), into which, according to legend, Amerindians pursued by the Spanish dropped bags of gold, although no-one has ever found anything of value.

The real treasure of the lake, however, is the colourful range of birdlife and the wide range of fish species; conditions are also ideal for mosquitoes, so beware, particularly in summer. On the other side of the lake stands Guamá: the name derives from an Indian chief who incited a rebellion against the Spanish in the east of Cuba in the 1520s. Some 50 bungalows have been built on stilts, on 12 man-made mini-islands linked together with wooden bridges.

BAY OF PIGS

About 15km (8 miles) south of La Boca lies the infamous **Bahía de los Cochinos**, the Bay of Pigs, the scene of the invasion of Cuba by Americans and exiled Cubans in April 1961, which was one of the most spectacular events of the Cold War era and a military adventure that the Americans would probably prefer to forget.

Some 80 small monuments, lying beside the road to Playa Larga on the bay, ensure the bloody

Star Attraction
● Ciénaga de Zapata National Park

US assault remembered
In the village of Playa Girón on the Bahía de los Cochinos, the Museo de Girón (8am–noon, 1–5pm) documents the story of the foiled US invasion in 1961. Castro had been tipped off about the American plans to overthrow him, so he was not surprised when, on 15 April, US planes painted with the Cuban symbol bombed airfields near Havana, Santiago and other airports.

Two days later, a large force including CIA-trained Cuban exiles landed at the Bahía de los Cochinos, but this assault failed miserably against a much smaller army of poorly equipped Cuban militias.

America had thought that the Cubans would welcome them with open arms, but the truth was that most of them still supported the Revolution. A Sea Fury plane of the Cuban airforce stands outside the museum.

Bay of Pigs memorial

Map on pages 48–9

debacle is never forgotten. Giant posters dotted around the place show Castro, who personally masterminded the Cuban defence, in olive green uniform clutching his Kalashnikov machine gun, reminding visitors of this celebrated episode in Cuban history. **Playa Larga** has a fine sandy beach and a small hotel of the same name (*see page 125*).

As well as commemorating the US invasion in the ★ **Museo de Girón** (*see page 59*), **Playa Girón** (185km/114 miles) has a quiet beach nearby with diving facilities. The **Playa Girón** hotel (*see page 125*) is a popular base for bird-watchers come to see the array of sea birds in the salty lagoons to the west of the village.

Below: children on Plaza José Martí, Cienfuegos
Bottom: Cienfuegos cathedral

CIENFUEGOS

Via Yaguaramas and Rodas and on to ★ **Cienfuegos**, the capital of the province of the same name (274km/170 miles). The historic town (pop. 137,000) lies in **Jagua Bay**, a natural harbour with a bottleneck opening about 300m (330yds) wide connecting it with the Caribbean.

There was a settlement here in the 16th century and from 1751 a sugar mill, but the town was not actually founded until 1819. At that time, black slaves working in the sugar plantations out-numbered whites, and although the Spanish gov-

ernor, José Cienfuegos, did not regard this imbalance as particularly threatening, he induced French settlers from Bordeaux, New Orleans and Florida to the region with free transport and land.

Cienfuegos rapidly developed as the centre of a very busy region. Its modern harbour has the largest sugar loading station in the world. In favourable conditions, up to 1,200 tons of sugar per hour can be loaded, and the warehouses can store up to 90,000 tons. Not only sugar, but also brandy, tobacco, tropical fruits and cement have contributed to the town's prosperity.

In the 1980s, plans for the Juragua reactor here, similar to that at Chernobyl, were drawn up by Soviet scientists. After 10 years of construction, however, Cuba's only attempt at generating nuclear power was shelved due to the poor economic situation and the break up of the Soviet Union.

PLAZA JOSE MARTI

The chimneys and factories in the newer part of Cienfuegos do not detract from the charm of the old town. In 1815, only a few years after it was founded, it was devastated by a cyclone, but was rebuilt in perfect chequerboard style. At its heart lies the neatly tended ★ **Plaza José Martí**, with its white lions and richly ornamented buildings testifying to the wealth that the French settlers accumulated during the 19th century. On the square stands a ceiba tree (said to bring luck) and a music pavilion. The **cathedral** (1867) with its two unequal towers looks rather awkward.

The neoclassical ★ **Teatro Tomás Terry** (daily 9am–6pm) is, however, worthy of closer attention. Built in 1889 with seats for 900 people, three colourful mosaics depicting the arts adorn the facade. Apart from one or two uncertain stylistic features, the Venezuelan property developer and millionaire undoubtedly would have been well satisfied with the monument that his sons built in his memory.

A performance of *Aida* marked the theatre's opening, with Caruso and Sarah Bernhardt joining in the celebrations. Many Cuban hardwood

Star Attraction
● Cienfuegos

Watersports centre
The favourite beach of the inhabitants of Cienfuegos is called Playa Rancho Luna (15km/9 miles to the southeast on the road to Pasacaballo). Its appeal lies mainly in the diving boards just offshore. Facilities at the Faro de Luna Hotel *(see page 125)* include a diving centre, hire of water-skiing, catamaran and windsurfing equipment, a restaurant and the option of boat trips.

Teatro Tomás Terry

Map on pages 48–9

trees had to be felled to furnish the interior, and the golden ceiling in the auditorium is lavishly painted with heavenly scenes. Fully restored in 1965, the theatre is now back in use as a venue for cultural, social and political events in the province.

On the other side of the square stands the **Capitolio**, though this is not to be compared with the one in Havana. The *Poder Provincial* (provincial government) is based here.

PALACIO DE VALLE

Below: Paseo del Prado
Bottom: Palacio de Valle

Up until the Revolution, racial segregation was clearly evident on the **Paseo del Prado** (Calle 37). One side of this grand boulevard was reserved for whites while blacks had to walk on the other side, and then only after they had finished their work.

The Prado runs right to the end of the **Punta Gorda** peninsula. We can now only guess at the riches amassed by the owners of the villas and gardens in this once grand, but now decaying quarter. Only the ★ **Palacio de Valle** (Calle 37 esq 0; daily 10am–5pm) reflects the US$1.5 million investments of its original owner, Asiclo Valle Blanco. This imposing palace is an imitation of Moorish architecture and several other styles – some impressive, some comical. Alfredo Colli, the Italian architect, spent four years up until 1917 trying to unite elements which did not really belong together. Climb up to the roof terrace for a magnificent view over the bay.

CASTILLO DE JAGUA

Just visible from the palace is the **Castillo de Jagua** (Tuesday to Sunday 9am–6pm), a small fortress with round towers at the entrance to the bay. Finished in 1745, this fortification was built to protect the town from pirates, who were constantly passing on their way to and from the Isla de la Juventud. At the Pasacaballo Hotel on the facing bank, boats wait to take visitors on the five-minute journey across to the small fishing village of Perché at the foot of the fortress. You can also get there by ferry from the port in Cienfuegos.

5: East of Eden

Cienfuegos – Sierra del Escambray – Topes de Collantes – Trinidad (82km/50 miles)

Map on pages 48–9

The Sierra del Escambray, which rises up behind Cienfuegos, appears to be covered with green wool; in fact, everything is green in this rainforest landscape. A mild aroma of coffee often hangs in the air – Cuba's best is grown on the 'crocodile's back'. On the south side of the mountains lies Trinidad, a charming colonial gem of a city.

As the roads are relatively good, you need not set aside a lot of time for this tour. If you want to stay longer in the region, you could explore the area by making a day trip to the provincial capital of Santa Clara.

Star Attraction
● Jardín Botánico

Sugar cane research
Before the Revolution, the Botanical Gardens outside Cienfuegos were run and used by Harvard University for Tropical and Subtropical Research. They are now administered by the Cuban Academy of Sciences.

BOTANICAL GARDENS

The ★★ **Jardín Botánico**, on the main road leading eastward out of Cienfuegos 15km (9 miles) from town, is a botanical gardens (daily 8am–4.30pm; tours in English, French, German and Portuguese) which was established at the beginning of the last century by Harvard University, who financed and administered it until the Revolution. Cuba's largest collection of flora, including some 2,400 different plants and trees from all over the world, grow on this 100-hectare (250-acre) site – there are 28

Bottom: bamboo at the Jardín Botánico

Map on pages 48–9

Cactus in bloom

different bamboos and 285 types of palm tree alone – and about 60 magnificent species of cactus are nurtured in the greenhouse.

Leonardo Alomá López, botanist and guide, has created an amazing botanical experience here: he can offer a creole hot dog made from the breadfruit tree and the sausage tree. He can hear bamboos growing – some put on 30cm (1ft) every day. And he is also a man with a wicked sense of humour – with the mother-in-law being his favourite target. One of his suggestions for getting rid of her is to make a boat out of jiquí wood. This wood is actually heavier than water, so any craft made out of it would sink straight to the bottom. He also has a deadly recipe for strychnine leaves *(strychnos nux vomica)*; you would die in three minutes.

SIERRA DEL ESCAMBRAY

Head back to the main road and follow it around the coast. On the left are the steep slopes of the ★★ **Sierra del Escambray**, whose highest peak is the 1,156-m (3,793-ft) Pico San Juan. In places, the hillsides are totally covered with *marabú* scrub. This hedging plant prevents erosion, but as far as farmers are concerned, it is a prickly, impenetrable bush, which spreads like a weed.

In March and April the coast road offers a bizarre spectacle. As part of their mating ritual,

Sierra del Escambray

thousands of crabs go walkabout on the road, with many ending up crushed beneath truck tires. The beneficiaries are the turkey vultures, who are not usually accustomed to finding their next meal served up to them quite so easily.

About 5km (3 miles) before Trinidad you will pass the turning up to the health resort of Topes de Collantes *(see page 68)*.

Star Attractions
● **Sierra del Escambray**
● **Trinidad**

TRINIDAD

Sugar barons, slaves and pirates have all left traces behind in ★★★ **Trinidad**, Cuba's fourth oldest, colonial town (pop. 40,000). As you stroll across the cobblestones in the central area, it is easy to imagine what it must have been like during the colonial era – slave traders parading their chained-up 'goods' through the streets, drinking water for sale in jugs, and an overpowering smell of dried fish. Hammered into the ground beside many of the buildings are cannon barrels – put there to protect corners of buildings from damage by high-wheeled coaches

Diego Velázquez founded this settlement in 1514 close to the Agabama and Tayabo rivers, which at that time yielded small quantities of gold. Initially, the Trinitarios made a living from smuggling, but in the 18th century, after they had been plundered several times themselves by pirates, the inhabitants turned to the more arduous but legal work of growing sugar cane, although, of course, it was the slaves who did all the hard work. Trinidad prospered with the sugar boom but when the trade shifted to Havana and Cienfuegos, and the end of slavery beckoned towards the end of the 19th century, the town sank as rapidly into insignificance as it had risen to prominence.

WORLD HERITAGE SITE

Today, the occasional mule-drawn cart passes by, driven by an old man in a broad straw hat. In the shadows a few men play dominoes, otherwise nothing much happens here. But at least the colonial architecture has survived the decline. In 1988,

Below: Plaza Mayor in Trinidad
Bottom: getting around town

Map on pages 48–9

Colonial delights

Visitors who are interested in colonial architecture, and the developments of the 18th and 19th centuries, will enjoy the **Museo de la Arquitectura Trinitaria** (Saturday to Thursday 9am– 5pm) on the northeast corner of Plaza Mayor. The house, which dates from 1738, once belonged to Sánchez Iznaga, at the time one of the richest men in Cuba. The colonnade and patio are perfect examples of colonial architecture and structural harmony.

UNESCO declared that Trinidad (along with the nearby Valle de los Ingenios) was to be conserved as a World Heritage Site, and many of the town houses have been lavishly restored. Vulgar signs and souvenir displays are against the law.

PLAZA MAYOR

The houses around the ★★★ **Plaza Mayor**, now almost all turned into museums, are immaculate. One of the most attractive, colonial-style ensembles is the **Museo de Arqueología y Ciencias Naturales Guamuhaya** (currently being restored, due to reopen early 2005) where, among the exhibits, are Indian stone tools, painted clay jugs and the skeleton of an Indian. The house that once stood in front of the yellow Rococo building here was the temporary home of the famous conquistador, Hernán Cortés (1485–1547), where he lived before he set off to conquer Mexico, frustrated by the meagre gold deposits in Cuba. A rather sparsely bristled conquistador toothbrush is displayed in the museum. Did the illustrious adventurer really once use it to clean his teeth?

Iglesia San Francisco

MUSEO ROMANTICO

Opposite the 18th-century **Parroquial Santísima Trinidad** (Church of the Holy Trinity), on the north corner of the square, stands the house where sugar baron Nicolás Brunet y Muñoz once lived, and which is now the ★★ **Museo Romántico** (Tuesday to Sunday 9am–5pm). On display here are exhibits of elegant hardwood furniture, quality Cuban workmanship, crystal chandeliers from Bohemia, faïences, and Sèvres and Meissen porcelain. Porcelain spittoons lie next to the armchairs in the lounge. The kitchen has huge pots standing on the hearth.

The sumptuous lifestyle of the 19th-century planters speaks volumes about the colonial era. The balcony on the first floor looks out over the Plaza Mayor, with its white fencing and English bronze greyhounds, the tiled roofs of the low houses and, to the right, the yellow-limed **Iglesia San Francisco** (1745), with a pretty bell-tower.

HUMBOLDT'S MUSEUM

The last of the museums on the Plaza Mayor, the ★**Museo Alejandro de Humboldt**, on the southeastern side, pays homage to the German explorer, Alexander von Humboldt (1769–1859). Although the globetrotting scientist spent only two days in the town in 1801, the Trinitarios have devoted this small collection to him. Humboldt made two visits to Cuba, one in 1800–1801 and another in 1804. The Cubans claim he made the 'second exploration' of their island; but he used a magnifying glass and surveying equipment, not a cross and a sword like his Spanish counterparts. Humboldt and his artist companion, Bonpland, disappeared into the woods to examine the soil and count the different grasses.

He wrote about his investigations in a book entitled *Political Essay on the Island of Cuba*, which was concerned not just with the island's fauna and flora, but also Cuba's socio-economic background and the vast chasm between rich and poor. Humboldt also had words to say about the island's economic mismanagement. Why did such a fertile country as Cuba need to import food? The mayor of Trinidad was not impressed by the German scientist, dismissing him as an ignorant man.

Further on at Calle Simón Bolívar 423 stands the Palacio Cantero, which houses the ★**Museo Histórico Municipal** (Saturday to Thursday

Star Attractions
- **Plaza Mayor**
- **Museo Romántico**

Below: the freedom of the street
Bottom: Humboldt plaque, outside his museum

SON CONOCIDAS YA LAS ANECDOTAS Y LAS HISTORIAS DE HEROES EXTRAORDINARIOS MUCHOS DE LOS CUALES DIERON SUS VIDAS INCLUSO COMBATIENTES QUE DURANTE AÑOS PERMANECIERON EN EL ANONIMATO, HEROES ANONIMOS CUYA VERDADERA IDENTIDAD NO PODIA SER DIVULGADA Y QUE ARROSTRARON ESE PAPEL DOBLEMENTE HEROICO DE DAR SU VIDA POR LA REVOLUCION SIN QUE EL PUEBLO SIQUIERA SUPIERA QUE QUIEN MORIA ALLI NO ERA UN MERCENARIO SINO UN REVOLUCIONARIO.

CMTE. EN JEFE FIDEL CASTRO
X ANIV. DEL MININT.

Map
on pages
48–9

> **Sugar slaves**
> About 50 or so large sugar mills or *ingenios* were built at the beginning of the 19th century to the east of Trinidad, in what is known as the **Valle de los Ingenios** (now under UNESCO protection). About 200 slaves with 12 supervisors used to work in each one, and towers such as the **Torre de Iznaga** (daily 9am–5pm) enabled guards to monitor every movement. From the top of the 45-m (148-ft) tower, they would see any irregularity and then, when necessary, sound the alarm. The slaves were kept locked up at night, but they sometimes managed to escape from their plantations. Escaped slaves were known as 'cimarrones'.

9am–5pm) which documents the history of the town. A sugar baron by the name of Cantero, who owned eight plantations and was once the richest man in Trinidad, used to live here.

EXCURSIONS

The 6-km (4-mile) long ★★ **Ancón Peninsula**, about 12km (7 miles) southwest of Trinidad, has long been a popular haunt for sun-worshippers. About 20 or so interesting underwater sights attract divers. Ancón is also the base for diving expeditions to the offshore Cayo Blanco. **Archipiélago de los Jardines de la Reina** is named in honour of Queen Isabel by Columbus 'Gardens of the Queen', the archipelago consists of almost 700 cays. For local fishermen, the tiny islands offer good pickings.

TOPES DE COLLANTES

Some 5km (3 miles) west of Trinidad is a right turn which snakes steeply into the Sierra del Escambray to the purpose-built health resort of ★ **Topes de Collantes**. Breathe deeply. The clear air here is said to protect against all known diseases. Established in the 1930s as a sanitarium for tuberculosis sufferers, the spa resort caters for health and fitness fans, with a vast array of facilities that include saunas, swimming pools and other sports and complementary therapies. Many visitors just come to see the **Caburní Waterfalls** and take walks through the pine forests. It is a beautiful, but quite stiff walk (three hours; guide compulsory – best booked a day in advance; tel: 042-540117). The road continues through spectacular scenery towards Manicaragua, where a left turn followed by another left turn will bring you to the glorious setting of ★**Lake Hanabanilla**. The large reservoir surrounded by hills is a great place to explore, with small waterfalls, caves, coffee plantations and hillside farmhouses. Boat trips depart from Hotel Hanabanilla on the eastern bank and give a glimpse of country life along the shores.

SANTA CLARA

It is a good 40km (25 miles) from the lake to ★★ **Santa Clara**. The provincial capital was once an Indian settlement and the Spanish did not arrive here until 1689. The town (pop. 300,000) may well have remained a backwater had not the Revolution fated it to be otherwise. Here, at the end of December in 1958, Che Guevara and 17 of his men ambushed an armoured train carrying Batista's troops. The rebels won the battle and the dictator fled from Cuba. Today, the wagons of the **Tren Blindado** (Monday to Saturday 8am–6pm, Sunday 8am–noon) house an exhibition of the event.

CHE'S FINAL RESTING PLACE

In the **Plaza de la Revolución** on the other side of town is a bronze statue of Che, and below is the ★★ **Mausoleo** (Tuesday to Saturday 8am–9pm, Sunday 8am–5pm) where Che's remains were brought with great ceremony in December 1997 to lie with those of his fellow Revolutionaries.

A non-Revolutionary attraction of Santa Clara is the excellent ★ **Museo de Artes Decorativas** (Monday, Tuesday and Thursday 9am–noon, 1–6pm, Friday and Saturday 1–6pm, 7–10pm, Sunday 6–10pm), full of 19th-century furniture displayed in a fine colonial building in Parque Vidal in the town centre.

Star Attractions
- Ancón Peninsula
- Santa Clara
- Mausoleo

Above: Che in bronze
Below: leisurely travel in Santa Clara

Map below

Below: uptown girls

6: Santiago de Cuba

For admirers of Cuba's Revolutionary heroes, Santiago at the eastern end (Oriente) of the island is hallowed ground. Almost all the independence movements in the history of Cuba have started here. Whether it was to do with exploitation by the colonial powers, slavery or American influence, the Santiagueros were always prepared to fight for *libertad*. The faces of the people radiate with pride and defiance.

One intrepid freedom fighter, Antonio Maceo, was born here, as too was the patriotic poet, José María Heredia. In fact, Santiago is sometimes described as the 'Cradle of the Revolution' or the 'heroic city'.

SECOND-LARGEST CITY

Despite the self-confidence of its inhabitants, Cuba's second-largest city has a rather provincial air compared with Havana. As one of the centres of the slave trade, the coffee plantation economy and later the chemical industry, it has been more difficult here than anywhere else to create a

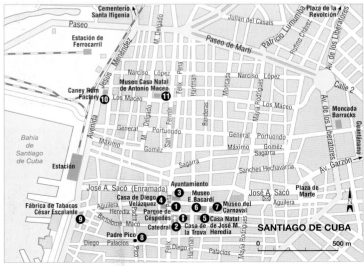

SANTIAGO DE CUBA

cohesive community. The interests of the rebels and the traditionalists, the plantation owners and the slaves, have always proved irreconcilable.

Relations with Havana have sometimes been strained too. It is not just the fact that the Orientales have traditionally been more pro-government than the Habaneros; it still rankles slightly with Santiago's townsfolk that in 1552 the status of capital city was taken from them after barely 30 years. Many, though, have gone to the capital looking for work.

THE OLD TOWN

No other place in Cuba exhibits that infectious Caribbean *joie de vivre* more than Santiago de Cuba. Spanish, French and African cultures have intermingled in this attractively located spot to create a lively and colourful Cuban cocktail.

The magnificent centrepiece of the **Old Town** is the ★★ **Parque de Céspedes ❶**, which acquired its name from the same freedom fighter *(see page 85)* who stands over the Plaza de Armas in Havana. The finest square in Santiago has witnessed some of the principal events in Cuban history: the Spanish established the headquarters of their colonial empire here, and relinquished power to the US in 1898 here too, after a short battle – Cuba was Spain's last colony.

Then, on 1 January 1959, thousands of jubilant people gathered in this square to pay homage to the victorious *guerrilleros* and hear the rebel leader, Fidel Castro *(see page 25),* proclaim that the Revolution had succeeded. The shady square with its stone benches is now a quiet and peaceful spot where, at the weekend, children can enjoy rides in small goat-drawn carts.

Overlooking the park is the **Catedral de Santa Ifigenia ❷** (daily 8am–noon, 5–7pm), the symbol for Santiago. The original building dating from 1528 was destroyed by an earthquake in 1678. Once restored, it was burnt down by the English in 1762 and struck by another serious earthquake in 1852. Work on a new cathedral started at the beginning of the 20th century. The finely carved choir

Star Attraction
● **Parque de Céspedes**

> **Double takes**
> Walking around Santiago can be confusing at times as some of the city's streets have several names. However, there is plenty to see so it's well worth taking a few days to explore, although it is best to avoid walking alone at night.

Below: Carlos Manuel Céspedes
Bottom: Catedral de Santa Ifigenia

Map on page 70

stalls are worth a look. It is supposed to contain the remains of the founder of the city, conquistador Diego Velázquez, but they have never been found.

Opposite the cathedral stands the **Ayuntamiento ❸** (Town Hall), seat of the *Poder Popular* (Popular Council); Fidel Castro was standing on one of its blue balconies when he announced the ending of the Batista era. This attractive colonial style building with its colonnaded portal is not open to the public. It is a reconstruction of the 17th century original.

CASA DE DIEGO VELAZQUEZ

From 1522 Velázquez, the first governor, lived near Céspedes Park. His residence, the ★★ **Casa de Diego Velázquez ❹**, in Andalusian Mudéjar style, is one of the oldest surviving buildings in Cuba. It has been carefully restored and, since 1971, has been a museum of colonial furniture and furnishings (Saturday to Thursday 9am–1pm, 2–4.30pm, Friday 2–4.30pm).

Exhibits include furnishings and decorations from the 16th to the 19th centuries. These give an insight into the luxurious lifestyles of the slave-owning aristocracy, who amassed huge wealth from the sugar and coffee plantations and copper mining. One particularly interesting item is the *tinajero*, a water filter in a mahogany stand – a block of porous limestone cleans the water as it passes through.

The ★ **Hotel Casa Granda** on the north side of the square radiates colonial grandeur, too. In true Cuban style, you can sit in a rocking chair on the verandah and quietly observe what is going on in the park. The best place to sit and observe the square, or head up to the 5th floor roof-terrace bar.

ENRAMADA AND CALLE HEREDIA

Running parallel to Parque de Céspedes is the **Enramada** (Calle José A. Saco), a busy thoroughfare and Santiago's main shopping street. It perfectly reflects the everyday life of all Cubans: shop-window displays are concerned

The busy Enramada

only with essential items and don't seek to arouse a longing for the unnecessary. The colours and illuminated advertisements date from the pre-Revolutionary era.

There is culture for all in Calle Heredia: go east along it from Parque de Céspedes. Musicians get together with the tourists in the ★ **Casa de la Trova** (Heredia 208, 11am–midnight). Paintings and photos on the walls are a reminder of its early, more spontaneous days and *Son* songs can be heard from midday onwards. There is always something going on here. Admission is US$1 and rum is served to visitors for US dollars.

JOSE MARIA HEREDIA

Just a few houses away stands the ★ **Casa Natal de José María Heredia** ❺ (Heredia 260 e/ Hartmann y Pío Rosado; Tuesday to Saturday 9am–8pm, Sunday 9am–2pm). José Heredia (1803–39) spread his ideas on national independence through verse, which greatly irked his Spanish colonial masters. He led a short and sorrowful life and much of it was spent in exile. His birthplace has a fine inner courtyard, where poetry readings and concerts are often held. Poetry workshops are on Thursday and Friday at 5pm.

Diagonally opposite is the **Museo Emilio Bacardí** ❻ (Monday noon–9pm, Tuesday to Saturday

Star Attraction
● Casa de Diego Velázquez

Dancing in the Calle
On Saturday and Sunday nights Calle Heredia breaks out into music fever and takes on a street carnival atmosphere, as musicians, dancers, mime artists and magicians 'put on a show' – anyone can join in, of course…

Below: Casa de la Trova
Bottom: Casa Natal de José María Heredia

Map on page 70

9am–9pm, Sunday 9am–1pm). Don Emilio, a member of the famous rum dynasty, founded the museum in 1899 with a collection that has nothing to do with his company's past, but is concerned with archaeology, colonial art and local history. He was Santiago's first mayor, and this is Cuba's oldest museum.

Nearby, another museum, the small ★ **Museo del Carnaval** ❼ (Heredia 303 esq Pío Rosado; Tuesday to Sunday 9am–5pm; 4pm Afro-Cuban music; closed Monday), documents the history of the Cuban carnival. Terrifying masks, extravagant costumes, posters and photos convey an impression of the riotous excitement that the hot-blooded Santiagueros stage along Avenida Garzon, Calles Trocha, Martí and Santa Ursula from 21–27 July.

Below: traditional transport
Bottom: casual observers

PADRE PICO

A detour to the west, via Calle Pío Rosado and then right into Calle Joaquín Castillo Duany, takes you to the harbour, but on the way you cross ★ **Padre Pico** ❽, an attractive street with a flight of steps that links the upper and lower town. It was in this district that most of the French coffee barons escaping from Haiti first settled. Santiagueros sit on the cobbled steps and play cards or dominoes, and the view from the top is fantastic.

TOBACCO AND RUM FACTORIES

If you are not intending to go to Pinar del Río *(see page 54)*, the home of the best tobacco in the world, visit the recently restored **Fábrica de Tabacos César Escalante** ❾ at 703 Avenida Jesús Menéndez, opposite the harbour (tel: 0226-22366; Monday to Saturday 9am–5pm).

A few hundred metres to the north along the same road stands the **Caney Rum Factory** ❿ – a bitter-sweet aroma emanates from the distillery. It is said that the vapours given off by the sugar cane brandy are an aid to good health. The hall where the workers used to process cane for the Bacardí dynasty is still in use, but now after the plant was nationalised following Castro's victory their labours benefit the Revolution and the people. When the political system changed, the trademarks changed too (rum under the Bacardí label is now made in Puerto Rico). In the bar, visitors may sample and buy the rum.

ANTONIO MACEO'S BIRTHPLACE

On the way to the Plaza de la Revolución in the north of the city, it is worth taking a detour to the **Museo Casa Natal de Antonio Maceo** ⓫ (Los Maceo 207 e/ Corona y Rastro; Monday to Saturday 9am–5pm, closed Sunday).

In the simple building where the mulatto General Antonio Maceo (1845–96) was born, the story of his role in the first and second Wars of Independence 1868–78 and 1895–death is recounted. Maceo, nicknamed the 'Bronze Titan', must have been a hothead of the first order. With a tiny army of 1,400 *mambises* (freedom fighters), he took on groups of the 182,000 soldiers of the Spanish army stationed on the island, winning numerous battles and skirmishes. After Maceo's death, (1896), the US intervened in the war in 1898 to protect their interests, both financial and strategic, in the island. They swiftly 'liberated' Cuba from the Spanish; the price they exacted was to submit the newly independent nation to the authority of an American military governor.

Bronze Titan
Antonio Maceo, hero of the Wars of Independence, rose from being a *mambis* (African Congo word for rebel) to being one of the most popular leaders of the struggle. The *mambises* were usually only armed with machetes for lack of guns, and went barefoot and barely clothed for lack of uniforms. He is said to have fought in 900 battles, been wounded 26 times, and survived many assassination attempts before being killed in battle by the Spanish in Pinar del Río province in 1896. His father and three of his brothers also perished in the wars.

Antonio Maceo remembered

Maps
on pages
70 & 82–3

Martí's mausoleum
In the Cementerio Santa Ifigenia, the tomb of Independence hero José Martí is the most visited. Six columns support the open octagonal structure, which enables natural light to shine on his sarcophagus inside, draped with the national flag, at any time of day. The six women carved on the outside of the mausoleum bear the symbols of Cuba's original six provinces.

Below: tomb of José Martí
Bottom: Moncada Barracks

SANTA IFIGENIA CEMETERY

Like every other large town in Cuba, Santiago has a **Plaza de la Revolución**. All visitors should take a quick look at this one at the end of Avenida de los Libertadores, to see the memorial to the local hero – a bronze equestrian statue of Antonio Maceo, framed by sharp machetes pointing skyward.

One of Cuba's most revered figures is the liberation fighter and poet, José Martí *(see page 38)*. He is buried in the ★ **Cementerio Santa Ifigenia** (daily 8am–6pm) on Avenida Crombet northwest of the city. The easiest way to get there is to take a taxi from the Plaza de la Revolución.

Martí's mausoleum is an impressive sight and you can see it for free from the car park but it is worth paying the US$1 admission fee to go into the cemetery, as Martí is not the only Cuban luminary to be buried here. The remains of Carlos Manuel de Céspedes *(see page 85)* are here, and there is a gravestone recording the lives and deaths of Emilio and Elvira Bacardí, although they are buried in Puerto Rico. The grave of Tomás Estrada Palma, the Cuban Republic's first president in 1902, is also here.

MONCADA BARRACKS

In the eastern part of the city stands the ★★ **Antiguo Cuartel Moncada**, the second-largest barracks on the island after the Columbia Barracks in Havana. Originally built between 1859–68, but rebuilt in 1938, after a fire, they have no architectural merit, but they do occupy a very important place in Cuban history. Batista took the garrison in 1952 and used it as a base for staging his military coup; as a symbol of the dictator's harsh regime, the barracks soon became a target for Fidel Castro and his fellow revolutionaries, who unsuccessfully attacked them on 26 July 1953 *(see page 25)*. The museum in the left-hand wing (Monday to Saturday 9am–7.30pm, Sunday 9am–1pm) houses a collection of objects and photographs that recall those turbulent times step by step. Bullet holes in the building's yellow facade filled in by Batista were reconstructed after the Revolution. The remainder of the barracks is used as a primary school.

EXCURSIONS

For a fine view over the town, the densely wooded Sierra Maestra and the Caribbean coast, it is worth making the trip up to ★★ **El Morro** fortress, 10km (6 miles) southwest of Santiago (daily 9am–7pm). Built between 1638 and 1642, on the cliffs above the entrance to the bottle-shaped Bahía de Santiago, to protect against buccaneers and other potential foes, it bears a striking resemblance to the El Morro fortress in Havana – it was designed by the architect, Juan Bautista Antonelli, the son of Giovanni Batista Antonelli, who designed the Morro in Havana. However, it was destroyed in 1662 by an English expedition commanded by Sir Christopher Myngs, in which the Welshman Henry Morgan (*circa* 1635–88) took part, and rebuilt between 1663 and 1710.

Inside the fortress is a display on the various pirates, corsairs, freebooters and buccaneers that once roamed these seas. In the armoury is an unusual device used to lift the heavy iron cannonballs up to the cannons on the battlements.

The story of piracy in the Caribbean starts at the time when buccaneers hunted down the

Star Attractions
● **Antiguo Cuartel Moncada**
● **El Morro**

Below and bottom: El Morro Fortress, inside and out

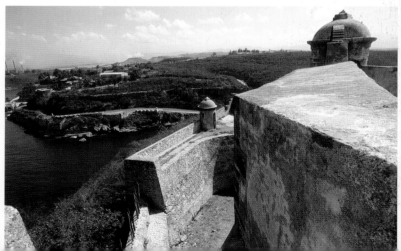

Maps on pages 70 & 82–3

treasures of the Spanish Main and ends with accounts of modern piracy, which, not surprisingly, focus on American policies in the region.

BOAT TRIPS AROUND THE BAY

A boat trip around the ★★ **Bahía de Santiago**, which cuts deep into the jagged rocks of the Sierra Maestra, is worth taking – boats usually leave every hour from the Punta Gorda jetty or from the Ciudamar jetty, 2km (1 mile) down the road from El Morro. Initially, a few fishing families settled on Socapa Point which juts out into the bay. Later, a few wooden summer houses were built, but although they have suffered badly from the elements, the area still has some of the charm of the New Orleans' French Quarter: the band of French planters who arrived here after fleeing from the slave rebellion in Haiti have left their traces.

In the middle of the Bahía de Santiago lies Cayo Granma, which before the Revolution was named Cayo Smith after an English slave dealer. Stop off for a seafood meal in the Rumbos restaurant. Some 1,400 people live on the island, but their view over to Santiago is not very pretty. Thick palls of yellowy-black smoke rise from the oil-fired power stations and other industrial complexes.

Bottom: Bahía de Santiago, and Cayo Granma

EL COBRE

About 25km (16 miles) west of Santiago, near Melgarejo in the heart of the Sierra Maestra, lies ★★ **El Cobre**, a place of pilgrimage. Copper *(cobre)* has been mined here since the 16th century, but never very productively. A white basilica stands like a heavenly apparition at the top of the wooded hill. Depending on your faith, it reveres either the Virgen de la Caridad del Cobre (the dark-skinned, miracle-performing Virgin of Charity), or the Goddess Ochún of the Santería sect *(see page 103)*.

According to legend, in 1606, three fishermen found a small wooden statue in the Bahía de Nipe on the north coast of the island, and brought it here. In 1916, Pope Benedict XV declared it to be a sacred relic. Now the faithful bring votive offerings and lay them at the feet of the Virgin – flowers, usually yellow, or jewellery, medals, cuddly toys and, more than anything else, pieces of lead shaped into parts of the body, which are intended to support the plea to the Virgin for a cure.

Sacrifices have included Hemingway's Nobel Prize medal for *The Old Man and the Sea*, as well as a golden lucky charm, which Fidel Castro, the *Máximo Líder* (Great Leader) was given by his mother. Pope John Paul II bequeathed a gold rosary to the statue in a ceremony attended by thousands when he visited Santiago in 1998.

THE GRANJITA SIBONEY

Just before Siboney, 17km (11 miles) to the east of Santiago, lies yet another shrine to the Revolution – and one that is always included on any sightseeing tour. The **Granjita Siboney** (Monday 9am–1pm, Tuesday to Sunday 9am–5pm) was a secret meeting place for the revolutionaries of the '26 of July Movement', where they planned their attack on the Moncada Barracks, but the authorities were always led to believe it was a chicken farm.

The house is directly beside the main road, and the rebels had to move around in total silence when they brought weapons here, in order to

Star Attractions
- **Bahía de Santiago**
- **El Cobre**

Below and middle: El Cobre basilica inside and out
Bottom: Granjita Siboney

Map
on pages
82–3

Good beaches

To the east of Santiago and into Parque Baconao are a number of good beaches tucked away between the rocky headlands. They include the Playas Arroyo de la Costa, Siboney, Juraguá, Damajayabo and Bocajagua. Most of them have fine sand and slope gently to the sea, but rocks are never far from the surface, so it's a good idea to wear something on your feet.

Above: dinosaurs in combat
Below: Baconao beach

avoid being overheard by the vigilant patrols. Their uniforms were stored above a false ceiling and their guns were hidden in the small well, still visible in the garden. Documents, photos, weaponry and the personal effects of the fighters are on display in the house.

GRAN PIEDRA NATIONAL PARK

To the north of Siboney lies ★ **Gran Piedra National Park** (about 28km/17 miles east of Santiago). Flourishing in the foothills of the Sierra Maestra are coffee, mangos and guava trees, plus 15 different types of fern. Accessible via steps, the 1,214-m (3,981-ft) summit of **Gran Piedra** provides a wonderful panorama. A dirt track at the bottom leads to ★ **La Isabelica** coffee plantation (daily 8am–4pm).

At the beginning of the 19th century, the estate belonged to Frenchman Victor Constantin, who had fled Haiti along with other coffee growers when the slaves revolted in 1795. The restored complex, with residence, warehouse, tools and coffee processing equipment, demonstrates the huge gulf between master and slave.

PARQUE BACONAO

Close to the coast, a further 20km (12 miles) eastwards, lies the **Parque Baconao**, which was opened in 1984 and has been declared a Biosphere Reserve by UNESCO. This 800-sq km (308-sq mile) recreation area is very popular with Cubans. One of the highlights is ★ **El Valle de la Prehistoria** (daily 8am–5pm), where a collection of 227 life-sized cement dinosaurs and pleistocene mammals provides an endless source of fascination for youngsters, especially since the film *Jurassic Park*. They were created in 1983 by prisoners as Cuba's answer to Disneyland and took seven years to make.

Just to the east is the **Conjunto de Museos de la Punta** (daily 8am–5pm) comprising several museums containing classic cars, archaeological artefacts, paintings, ceramics, folk costumes, stamps and cigar seals. Other attractions in the area include **El Mundo de la Fantasia** (a Disneyland-style park) and the dolphin shows at the **Aquario Baconao**.

Map
on pages
82–3

7: The Wild Oriente

Santiago de Cuba – Sierra Maestra – Manzanillo – Bayamo – Santiago de Cuba (450km/280 miles without detours)

Star Attraction
● Sierra Maestra

The Oriente, as the Cubans call the eastern end of their island, is wild. But not only is the mountain backdrop of the Sierra Maestra stark and austere, the people too are renowned for a rebellious streak. No other part of Cuba has such a long list of battles and uprisings.

Below: children in Bayamo
Bottom: beach life beneath the Sierra Maestra

The journey along the coast is a fascinating experience: green mountains and turquoise blue seas with tall royal palms in between. Most of the houses are *bohíos (see page 99)* and the mule is the best means of transport in such rough terrain. It is unusual to encounter human life outside the villages. Only in Manzanillo, the birthplace of the Cuban music *son*, do things get livelier.

Plenty of time is needed for this route – it may look short on the map, but with the hair-pin bends and rough tracks it could take three hours to cover 100km (60 miles).

Shrimp fishermen

THE SIERRA MAESTRA

Cuba's highest mountain range, the ★★★ **Sierra Maestra**, envelopes Santiago de Cuba on both sides, extending eastwards from near Cabo Cruz in the west for about 240km (150 miles). The northern hillsides are suitable for settlements and coffee plantations but, along the south-facing side, which is virtually uninhabitable, steep mountain slopes alternate with quiet bays. Agaves bloom, the aroma of eucalyptus wafts through the air, and prickly cacti border the roads. After about 60km (37 miles) on the coast road, which offers some fine views over mountains and ocean, an opportunity for a dip in the sea presents itself just before Chivirico, at the **Playa Sevilla**.

PICO TURQUINO

After a further 60km (37 miles), **Pico Turquino** (1,972m/6,468ft), the highest mountain in Cuba,

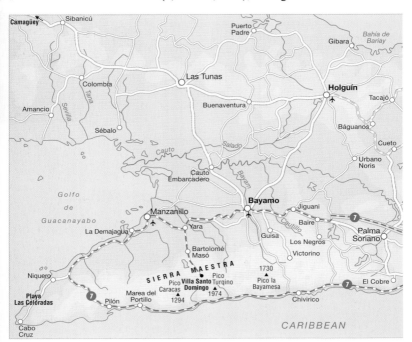

comes into view on the right. Guides lead hikes along the many beautiful trails around the mountain, although sometimes the path up Pico Turquino itself is closed. Various types of fern thrive at higher altitudes between the rocks and boulders, lower down, mahogany, cedar and trumpetwood trees grow. Wild orchids hang from the branches. Look out for the indigenous land snails *(polimitas)* with their shells of many colours and the *greta cubana* butterfly, with translucent wings edged in black and red.

This terrain was ideal for the guerrilla war that Fidel Castro started here in 1956 *(see page 26)*. His bush fighters could suddenly appear from nowhere and confront the government soldiers, then vanish again just as quickly. Even Batista's intelligence planes were outwitted.

It was in the Sierra Maestra in 1957 that Castro gave his first interview, after Batista had announced that the rebel leader had died in the landing of the

Fidel Castro with his brother, Raúl, and Camilo Cienfuegos, in the Sierra Maestra, 1957

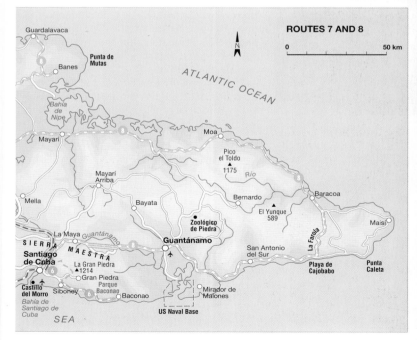

ROUTES 7 AND 8

0   50 km

ATLANTIC OCEAN

Guardalavaca
Punta de Mutas
Banes
Bahía de Nipe
Mayari
Moa
Pico el Toldo ▲1175
Río
Mayarí Arriba
Mella
Bayata
Bernardo
Baracoa
El Yunque ▲589
Zoológico de Piedra
Maisí
La Maya
Guantánamo
Guantánamo
SIERRA MAESTRA
Santiago de Cuba
La Gran Piedra ▲1214
Gran Piedra
San Antonio del Sur
La Farola
Castillo del Morro
Siboney
Parque Baconao
Baconao
Mirador de Malones
Playa de Cajobabo
Punta Caleta
Bahía de Santiago de Cuba
SEA
US Naval Base

Map on pages 82–3

cabin cruiser *Granma* at Playa de las Coloradas in December 1956. After hiding in the mountains for several months, Castro spoke to Herbert L. Matthews of the *New York Times* in order to prove that he was still alive. The Cuban people's support for the guerrillas grew dramatically after that.

Devotees of Revolutionary sites can make a detour to the **Playa Las Coloradas**, 20km (12 miles) south of **Niquero** towards Cabo Cruz. A monument on the beach further south marks the actual landing place of the famous cabin cruiser. **Alegría de Pío**, in the mountains behind, was where the *guerrilleros,* including Fidel Castro, were nearly wiped out during their first encounter with Batista's troops.

Below: models of varying vintage
Bottom: Moorish-style architecture in Manzanillo

MANZANILLO

Once you have reached the port of ★ **Manzanillo** (252km/156 miles) on the eastern coast of the Golfo de Guacanayabo, the mountains disappear from view. The 100,000 or so inhabitants of this town cannot resist the special rhythm of *son (see page 102)*. The pattern for the rhyming eight-syllable verses, originated in the hills of Oriente outside Manzanillo.

The Moorish-style architecture in the city centre is fascinating. It was during the 16th century, to the southwest of the present town centre, that

the Spanish burnt alive the Arawak *cacique* (chief), Hatuey, who had steadfastly resisted the Spanish oppression of the Taíno people. Before his death, the conquistadors tried to convert him to Christianity; when the priest tried to baptize him, the Indian asked if there were any Christians in Heaven, and when told that there were, he said he'd rather die a pagan.

YARA

The road to Bayamo runs past swamp and rice fields back to the foothills of the Sierra Maestra. Some 23km (15 miles) east of Manzanillo is the town of **Yara**. After freeing his slaves at La Demajagua, near Manzanillo, Carlos Manuel Céspedes and his followers arrived here on 11 October 1868 and fought their first battle against the Spanish, an event recalled by the monument on the main square. The town is famous for the Yara Declaration in which Céspedes proclaimed Cuban Independence.

Heading south from Yara, the road leads past Bartolomé Masó and up to ★★ **Villa Santo Domingo** in the Sierra Maestra. This is the main base for visiting the **Gran Parque Nacional Sierra Maestra**, where there are great hiking possibilities. An incredibly steep concrete access road leads up as far as Alto del Naranjo, from where a two- to three-day trek leads all the way to the south coast, taking in the Pico Turquino on the way. An easier excursion from the pass is westward for 3km (2 miles) along a clearly marked trail to the ★★ **Comandancia de la Plata**, Castro's Revolutionary headquarters, where alongside his residence is a museum, field hospital, command post, and the original site of Radio Rebelde *(see page 121)*. No cameras allowed into the Comandancia de la Plata itself, halfway along the trek, they will be taken from you and looked after.

BAYAMO

★**Bayamo** (322km/200 miles) is the lively capital of Granma province (pop. 125,000), where

Star Attraction
● Comandancia de la Plata

Freedom fighter
Enthused by Thomas Jefferson's ideas on liberty, the plantation owner Carlos Manuel de Céspedes (born 1819 in Bayamo) became a fierce proponent of freedom and equality. One of Céspedes' aspirations was the abolition of slavery, an objective that his American counterpart never envisaged.

On 10 October 1868, he released the slaves that he kept on his La Demajagua plantation near Manzanillo, thus triggering the First War of Independence, mainly fought in the Oriente. With military leaders, Antonio Maceo and Máximo Gómez, Céspedes fought on until 1874 when he met his death in a Spanish ambush.

The Sierra Mestra

Map
on pages
82–3

it would be easy to spend a whole day. The fleet of horse-drawn *coches* provide an efficient taxi service and also give a calm and leisurely atmosphere to the town but, in fact, a Revolutionary spirit has existed here for centuries.

The conquistador Diego Velázquez founded the settlement in 1513 on the navigable Río Bayamo. An Indian uprising took place 17 years later, and after that, it was the African slaves in the unproductive gold mines who rebelled. A brisk trade in smuggling brought the inhabitants into conflict with the Spaniards' strict economic regime. Not surprisingly, Céspedes encountered fertile ground with his ideas for independence, and Martí's struggle against the colonial masters also had its roots here. From then on, Bayamo was regarded as the 'cradle of nationalism'.

Worth a visit is the ★ **Casa Natal Carlos Manuel de Céspedes** (Maceo 57; Tuesday to Friday 9am–5pm, Saturday 9am–2pm, 8–10pm, Sunday 10am–1pm, closed Monday), the birthplace of the progressive 'father of all Cubans'. This colonial-style villa contains furniture and documents that date from the late 19th century and exhibits about Céspedes' eventful life.

Next door is the **Museo Provincial** (Tuesday to Sunday 8am–6pm, Saturday 10am–2pm; closed Monday), which is housed in impressive neoclassical premises and includes exhibits of archaeological finds, which help to build up a picture of the city's past.

Below: Casa Natal Carlos Manuel de Céspedes
Bottom: Catedral San Salvador

SAN SALVADOR

The attractive ★ **Catedral San Salvador** near the main square, sometimes described as the 'Church of Fate', is one of the oldest churches in Cuba. When colonial troops stormed Bayamo during the First War of Independence in 1869 to put down the rebels, the inhabitants set their town on fire and fled to the hills. The remains included the small 'Chapel of the Sufferings of Mary' with a laminated wooden altar, baroque sculptures of Cuban fruit and the stone font at which Céspedes was baptised.

8: In the footsteps of Columbus

Santiago de Cuba – Baracoa – Holguín – Guardalavaca (542km/336 miles without detours)

Map on pages 82–3

Contrasts abound on the way to paradise. The province of Guantánamo is in places so parched that not even cacti can survive the harsh environment. On the other side of the Baracoa mountains, the countryside comes alive with lush, green rain forests. Today's visitors are as astounded as Christopher Columbus must have been when, in October 1492, he first set foot on the island.

Mountains, tropical vegetation, the blue of the Caribbean and the palm-lined beaches in deserted bays – hardly anything has changed since the day he came ashore. This is because the coast road was not built until the 1960s. Before then access was by boat. Motor vehicles have only appeared here relatively recently and the people still live very simply, tending their fields with hoes and primitive ploughs and carrying produce on mules.

US GUANTANAMO

Millions of people will be familiar with the famous song *Guantanamera*, but few will realise that its origins are Cuban or that the words were written by the Cuban hero, José Martí *(see page*

Cuban hit

One of the world's most familiar songs – *Guantanamera* or the 'girl from Guantánamo' – was initially a poem written by the Cuban hero José Martí in his collection *Versos sencillos*. It was set to the music, composed by Joseíto Fernández, many years after his death:

'*I am a sincere man
from the land of the palm tree
and before I die I wish to sing
these heart-felt verses.
With the poor of the land I want
to share a fate
and the mountain stream pleases me
more than the sea.*'

Baracoa coastline

Map
on pages
82–3

Danger
It's important to heed the barbed wire and warnings to keep out of the US military base, as it is heavily mined. However, it is said that the mines are in the process of being dismantled.

Below: life in the slow lane
Bottom: Revolution sculpture in Guantánamo

87). Nearly as famous as the girl from **Guantánamo** (85km/135 miles) is the now notorious US base near the town, which was established in 1903. This vast complex, 110 sq km (36 sq miles) in area, houses some 5,000 US soldiers and prisoners from Afghanistan and Iraq that the US is holding without trial. The presence of the base is greatly resented by the Cuban government and Cuban people.

Fortunately for the Cubans, the original lease for perpetuity was changed in 1934 to a 99-year agreement. So they will just have to wait patiently until 2033, as Uncle Sam is unlikely to leave willingly before then.

Visitors can safely give the town of Guantánamo a miss, but for those who want a glimpse of the base, the best view is from Los Malones lookout point, about 24km (15 miles) east of Guantánamo on the Baracoa road. You need to arrange a visit in advance – buy a US$5 voucher from one of the travel agencies in central Santiago. You must get to the checkpoint for Malones between 10am and 2pm to be allowed through.

LA FAROLA

The little town of Baracoa is definitely worth a visit, and is an easy trip from Guantánamo along *La Farola,* a road winding up the hillside with

more than 261 bends. The onward journey to Guardalavaca, however, is quite tricky. It is an absolutely spectacular route, with the rain forest creeping across the road; unfortunately, however, this 'road' is no more than a pot-holed sand track, and those in a hurry are advised to take the helicopter from Baracoa.

Star Attractions
● Baracoa
● El Yunque (see overleaf)

BARACOA

The journey to ★★★ **Baracoa** along the coast road is a scenic delight: on the right the Caribbean Sea glinting in the sun, on the left limestone rocks dropping steeply down to the sea. After 236km (146 miles), you will come to what was the first Spanish settlement on Cuba, now expanded to a town of about 50,000 inhabitants.

Below: bust of Chief Hatuey, Baracoa
Bottom: the nearby coast

Founded in 1512 by Diego Velázquez, Baracoa was the Cuban capital for three years, and in 1518 the first church on Cuban soil was consecrated as a cathedral there. Its replacement is the **Catedral de Nuestra Señora de la Asunción** (1833) by the Plaza Independencia (also known as Parque Central). In front of the cathedral is the bust of the *cacique*, Hatuey, who was burned at the stake in 1512 *(see page 85)*. The cathedral's most interesting treasure is the controversial Cruz de la Parra, a cross which many once believed Christopher Columbus brought with him on his second voyage of discovery. It may be connected with Columbus, but it was actually made in Cuba of a local wood.

Baracoa itself is a sleepy little town, but its attractive colonial buildings make it a very appealing spot. In order to breathe new life into the community, the Government is promoting tourism here. At the southeast entrance to the town, the Fuerte Matachín houses the **Museo Municipal** (daily 8am–noon, 2–6pm), which provides a good overview of local history. Another Spanish fort, the **Fuerte de la Punta**, has watched over the harbour entrance at the northwest end since 1803. Good views from 'El Castillo' that dominates the centre of town – the town's main castle ramparts, are now converted into a hotel.

Map
on pages
82–3

EL YUNQUE

Guides will escort energetic climbers to the top of the 589-m (1,931-ft) ★★**El Yunque** table mountain behind the town. Other attractions include canoeing trips on the nearby **River Toa** and horseback rides to the cocoa plantations. There is also the verdant farm of **Finca Duaba**, 6km (4 miles) out on the road to Moa, which is designed to give visitors a taste of country life.

An unusual inhabitant of the Baracoa beaches is the *polymita picta* land snail. These colourful creatures do not occur anywhere else in the world, and the locals use the pretty shells to make jewellery, but don't be tempted to buy them – they're protected under both Cuban and international law (CITES). Some 20km (12 miles) northwest of Baracoa at ★★★**Maguana** is one of the most perfect palm-fringed white beaches in Cuba.

Below: warm smile in Holguín
Bottom: Holguín poster

HOLGUIN

From Baracoa to Báguanos, where the detour to Holguín begins, is a daunting 222km (137 miles). Include the 30km (19 miles) after the junction and the journey will take a good five hours.

Holguín is Cuba's fourth largest city (pop. 312,000). Situated at an important road junction, it is a prosperous place and looks set to become even better off as tourism develops and the inter-

national airport grows in importance. There are a number of public parks and pleasant squares, including **Parque Calixto García**, the main one, which has a statue of General Calixto García who captured Holguín from the Spaniards in 1872.

On the north side of the square is the ★ **Museo de Historia Provincial** (Monday to Friday 8am–9pm, Saturday and Sunday 8am–5pm), whose fascinating exhibits include the *hacha de Holguín* (Holguín axe found in 1860), an ancient indigenous ceremonial axe head carved in the likeness of a man and adopted as the symbol of the province. Another interesting museum is the **Museo de Ciencias Naturales Carlos de la Torre** (Tuesday to Sunday 9am–10pm; closed Monday) in the Calle Maceo, which keeps a collection of 7,000 exhibits, 4,000 of which are snail shells, including the colourful *polymita picta*, and over 100 stuffed birds.

Before covering the last few miles via Tacajó to Guardalavaca, make a detour to **Banes**, an interesting town built by United Fruit: here you'll find the ★★ **Museo Bani-Indocubano** (Calle General Marrero 305; Tuesday to Saturday 9am–5pm, Sunday 8am–noon, 2–5pm, also Friday–Sunday 7–9pm), the home of Taíno Indian culture where there are 1,000 sacred, decorative and everyday objects on display, just a small proportion of the 14,000 finds from the many recent excavations.

Nearby, in ★★★ **Chorro de Maíta**, is the largest Taíno burial ground in Cuba, dating from the 15th century, and a reproduction of a Taíno village.

GUARDALAVACA

★★ **Guardalavaca** (542km/336 miles) depends on tourism and is reminiscent of classic Caribbean tourist brochures: a bright blue sky, a turquoise sea lapping a beach of soft, white sand, pretty girls serving rum cocktails beneath gently swaying palms to the rhythmic sound of *son*. You can explore the coastline and hinterland by helicopter – it will even take you to some of the more remote beaches, such as the beautiful **Don Lino** and **Playa Blanca** to the west. For divers, a 300-m

Star Attractions
- **Maguana**
- **Museo Bani-Indocubano**
- **Chorro de Maíta**
- **Guardalavaca**

Roots of a dictator
The cruel dictator Fulgencio Batista was born in Banes into a poor family of cane-cutters. Ironically the most well-off family in the area were the Castros, and the older local people can still remember when Fidel and his brother Raúl came to dances in the town.

Playa Esmeralda near Guardalavaca

Map on page 93

The name game
The Isla de la Juventud has had a string of names over the past 500 years, but it acquired its present title in the 1970s when Cuba offered students from developing countries free education here in a bid to spread solidarity for the Revolution. At one time there were 60 boarding schools accommodating 150,000 young people – hence the name the 'Isle of Youth'. However, the economic problems of the 1990s put an end to this concentration.

(1,000-ft) long coral reef, similar to that of the Cayería del Norte, offers some incredible encounters with marine fauna and flora.

Further to the west is a place of great historic significance. On 28 October 1492, Christopher Columbus came ashore at the **Bahía de Bariay**, a small inlet. He was impressed by what he saw, but behind his enthusiasm was the hope that he would find gold here. It was, after all, the prospect of riches that motivated his journey into the unknown. A memorial here marks the meeting of the Old World with the New. The peninsula is now a protected park: the Parque Monumento Nacional Bariay (daily 9am–5pm).

9: The Islands and the Cayos

Hundreds of *cayos* or coral islands with snow-white beaches lie off the southern and northern coast of Cuba – and these are a veritable paradise for nature lovers, watersports enthusiasts and budding Robinson Crusoes. Many areas are unexplored and totally deserted, so the beaches here are truly idyllic. Dolphins dive, pelicans sun themselves and pink flamingos preen, tugging busily at their feathers. The sand is powdery and the water so soft that it feels as if it has been treated with fabric softener.

The beach at the Hotel Colony, Isla de la Juventud

ISLA DE LA JUVENTUD

The Isle of Youth, or ★★ **Isla de la Juventud**, is Cuba's largest offshore island and, as part of the Canarreos Archipelago, is situated only 70km (43 miles) off the southern coast. In the deep waters around the archipelago lie huge swathes of coral which offer divers some amazing sights. The Ciénaga de Lanier swamp belt divides up the fertile island, 3,060 sq km (1,180 sq miles) in area, into two quite distinct landscapes: mountains, plantations and settlements in the north, woodland in the south. With green hills, mango trees, coconut palms, citrus and pineapple groves, this is Cuba's orchard.

After the first Western explorers discovered the Caribbean, the 'Isla' was involved in some dramatic adventures – some of which have been adapted for portrayal on the cinema screen. From the 16th century onwards, the island was a hideaway and headquarters for pirates seeking to break the Spanish trade monopoly. It was certainly no accident that the most famous buccaneers and adventurers were of Dutch, English or French nationality. Anywhere else, thieves would have had their hands chopped off, but in these countries, pirates were rewarded with titles and feted as heroes.

In 1628, the Dutchman Piet Heyn robbed the Spanish of 15 million guilders, a deed for which he was showered with praise in his home country. It is not so widely known that Sir Francis Drake (1540–96), the famous British sea captain who defeated the Spanish Armada, spent the early part of his sea-going life in the Caribbean plundering gold-laden Spanish galleons on their

Star Attraction
● **Isla de la Juventud**

Below: market day in La Fé
Bottom: laid back locals

Map on page 93

way home from Peru and Mexico. John Hawkins (1532–95) used to fill his water tanks on the island, which was then called Parrot Island, as it was the habitat of many brightly coloured parrots, and he also repaired his ships there.

TREASURE ISLAND

The British buccaneer Henry Morgan, probably the most terrifying of all pirates, had a base for 700 men and 12 vessels on the Isla de la Juventud, and his repeated attacks on the ports of Santiago and Camagüey made him a rich man.

Not surprisingly, the island acquired the mysterious name of 'Isla del Tesoro' (Treasure Island) and it is said to have inspired Robert Louis Stevenson to write his famous novel of the same name in 1883. When it was made into a film, the producer chose this island as the location.

PRESIDIO MODELO

Catamarans for the Isla de la Juventud leave from Puerto Surgidero de Batabanó, 50km (31 miles) south of Havana (crossing: 3–5 hours). One catamaran leaves in the morning and returns in the evening. Cheap flights are also available and are a much better option. For details, enquire at hotels or travel agents.

Below: Nueva Gerona harbour
Bottom: sunset over the cayos

Nueva Gerona is the island's main town, and was founded by Spanish settlers fleeing from newly-independent American territories. Later, in the early 1900s, it was home to many settlers from the US. It is here where the lumberjacks and charcoal burners, the citrus plantation workers and marble quarrymen live, along with most of the other 68,000 islanders. The most interesting monument on the island is the ★★**Presidio Modelo** or Model Prison (Monday to Saturday 8am–4pm, Sunday 8am–noon) to the east of Gerona. Now a museum, it was a prison until 1967, with a reputation as fearsome as Alcatraz. Built for 6,000 convicts between 1926 and 1932 by the dictator Machado, it was modelled on the Joliet prison in Illinois. Its most famous inmate was Fidel Castro himself, who spent 19 months here as punishment for his part in the attack on the Moncada Barracks *(see page 76)*.

Another national hero, José Martí, also had some unhappy experiences on the island. As a result of some of his anti-colonial writing, he was brought here in 1870 and held for several years under house arrest in the **Finca El Abra**, 2km (1¼ miles) southwest of Gerona off the road to La Demajagua. Martí's bedroom and some personal belongings can be seen at this farm (Tuesday to Sunday 9am–5pm; closed Monday).

The sandy beach at **Bibijagua**, 8km (5 miles) to the east, owes its dark colour to the black marble which is quarried in the nearby Sierra de Cabales. The finest beach on the island is at **Punta del Este**, 59km (37 miles) to the southeast of Gerona; however, the ★★**indigenous cave paintings**, which were discovered in 1922, are the greatest attraction here. The walls and ceiling of the cave are covered with black and red pictographs. Experts believe that the circles are a form of solar calendar and the mysterious paintings on the ceiling represent stellar movements.

Star Attractions
● Presidio Modelo
● Indian cave paintings

Below: Presidio Modelo
Bottom: Finca El Abra

The Pirate Coast
Around the area known as the Costa de los Piratas (Pirates' Coast), in the spectacular diving waters off Punta Francés, are wrecks of Spanish galleons and pirate ships.

CABO FRANCES

The wonderful underwater scenery off **Cabo Francés** in the west of the island was discovered

Map
on page
97

After your blood...

Be warned: mosquitoes in search of fresh, human blood present a major hazard to anyone out of doors after 6pm. Come well supplied with insect repellent.

Below: dive shop badges
Bottom: sea and sun

in the 1950s. At the cape, Cuba's mainland shelf drops by over 1,000m (3,300ft), while water temperatures vary very little – from 25°C (77°F) in winter to 29°C (84°F) in summer. For aficionados, this remote peninsula, with its amazing coral reefs and colourful underwater fauna and flora, ranks among one of the world's best diving spots.

The International Scuba Diving Centre has designated 56 caves, crevices and passes for diving; as the area is now a marine reserve, diving is only permissible with an official guide. To overcome access difficulties, a diving station with restaurant, changing rooms and toilets has been erected out at sea and is linked to the shore by a long walkway. Snorkellers can also appreciate the beauty of the coral reefs. No other signs of civilisation are to be found at Punta Francés. The main base for divers is the Hotel Colony at the other side of the Ensenada de la Siguanea.

CAYO LARGO

Only 27km (17 miles) long, the narrow island, of ★★ **Cayo Largo** lies at the eastern end of the Canarreos Archipelago. Although it is much smaller than the Isla de la Juventud, it is much better equipped for tourism. The holiday centre, with six hotels at the heart of Cayo Largo, can offer access to an unspoilt natural environment,

with long, lonely sandy beaches for sun-wor-shippers, magnificent coral reefs for divers and a bird reserve for ornithologists.

The beaches at **Lindamar**, **Blanca**, **Cocos**, **Tortugas** on the south coast and **Luna** on the north coast offer very little protection from the sun. Probably the most popular beach is the **Playa Sirena**, which lies at the western tip of the island. This is where the sea is at its calmest. If you are walking along the seashore with bare feet, you will be struck by how powdery the sand is.

Anyone who is not a dedicated sun-wor-shipper or beach-walker will quickly get bored on this uninhabited island – a tour of the turtle farm in the holiday centre will not take long. Facilities at this mini-village include an information office, a diving club, doctor's surgery, a chemist, jeep hire and a taxi rank. Excursions into the surrounding area leave from Playa Sirena or from Marina Isla del Sol.

Star Attractions
● Cayos Largo and Coco

THE NORTHERN ISLANDS

More than 400 islands or *cayos* make up the Camagüey and Sabana archipelagos off the north coast of Cuba. Having measured the sand grains on the northeast Cayería coast at a minute 0.12mm in diameter, scientists believe them to be the finest in the world. The whole region has been designated as a nature and bird reserve, though in some parts tourism has encroached on to this island paradise. But once you are away from the hotels and bars you will soon find yourself alone with the sea and the sun. A 27-km (17-mile) causeway links the island of ★★ **Cayo Coco** (364 sq km/140 sq miles) with San Rafael on the mainland. The hotels are mainly along the coast, which is edged with white sand beaches. On tiny, neighbouring ★ **Cayo Guillermo**, a fishing haunt of Hemingway's (13 sq km/ 5 sq miles) to the west, there are now four hotels.

Art and Architecture

Unlike the Aztecs, the Mayas and the Incas, the Cuban indigenous groups did not build any temples or palaces. The architectural inheritance of the Taínos and Ciboneys are *bohíos*, simple peasants' huts, constructed principally from royal palms. Their leaves cover the roof, their trunks form the walls. When the Spanish arrived in the 16th century, they constructed buildings made of stone in the Iberian architectural style. Town halls and churches, palaces and residences were built around central, park-like squares.

When mention is made of the 'colonial style', it refers to the period from 1492 to 1898; over 400 years, this style manifested itself in many different ways. Many Cuban town centres are adorned with classical-style arcades, terraces and columns, and baroque influences are very limited.

BARROTES AND BALCONIES

In the 17th century, architects made further refinements to suit the climate. Openings with *persianas*, fan-shaped, moveable slats above the doors and windows, enabled the air to circulate, but at the same time reduced the intensity of the sunlight. Tall, unglazed windows which extended down to the floor allowed enough air to enter and were secured with attractive grilles, or *barrotes* which, carved initially from wood, were made of metal from the 19th century onwards. The resident, seated in a rocking chair a few steps above the pavement, could watch goings-on outside from behind the *barrotes*.

Narrow balconies on the first floor – invariably with ornate ironwork balustrades – were roofed and supported by pillars. From the safety of these *guardavecinos*, it was possible to keep an eye on the neighbours. This type of building, with its flat roofs and ochre tiles, evokes the atmosphere of medieval Spain.

In contrast to the stylish colonial architecture of their forbears, socialist-style dwellings look bleak. Almost all the residential blocks built after

Opposite: balcony in Old Havana
Below: church in Nueva Gerona
Bottom: Matanzas colonnade

Mudéjar palaces
During the 16th and 17th centuries, many palaces were built in the Moorish-influenced Mudéjar style. These had a simple, two-storey structure, often with horseshoe arches and a patio or inner courtyard, so all parts of the building enjoyed light, shade and air. The swinging patio doors or *mamparas* allowed a fresh breeze to blow inside.

Art at the roots
Afro-Cuban mythology influences Cuban culture profoundly, as seen in the paintings of Manuel Mendive (b.1944), Cuba's leading contemporary artist. His style, appreciated worldwide, is primitivist, whereas the work of Cuban-Chinese Flora Fong, another highly acclaimed artist, combines Caribbean colours with hints of her ethnicity.

Below: Revolutionary art

the Revolution are spartan, functional and unimaginative. But then, during the 1960s, the Government was only interested in building homes for the people.

ART

It was during the first part of the 20th century that Cuban art was brought to international notice, and Havana started to attract many foreign artists. However, the island's most famous painter, the surrealist Wilfredo Lam (1902–82), went to Europe where he attended the Academy of Art in Madrid with Salvador Dalí and was treated like a son by Pablo Picasso. Afro-Cuban spirituality radiates from Lam's brush strokes, and spectres, demons and eerie powers appear in many of his paintings. He was also greatly influenced by Picasso's Cubist ideas.

Another individualistic Cuban painter of this period was René Portocarrero (1912–85), whose expressive oils depicted versions of Havana and beautiful women.

With the Revolution a new kind of realist art emerged. Castro actively encouraged the arts with state sponsorship, but at the price of freedom of expression. Those who survived the extremes of censorship and official art – in recent years, many young artists have left the country after their work was confiscated for its dissident style – continue to paint in abstract forms.

Literature

Before the Revolution, few Cubans were able to read, let alone buy books. But Cuban authors have contributed greatly to the success of the state education system. Plays, poems and essays by national hero José Martí *(see page 38)* are very popular with Cubans – his uncomplicated style of writing has meant that his work is easily accessible to most.

The same is true of the mulatto poet, Nicolás Guillén (1902–89), who devoted much of his writing to Afro-Cuban themes, and some of his work can be recited to a drumbeat. He became a Communist while he was working as a journalist reporting the Spanish Civil War, and as a result had to live in exile while Batista was in power. Back in Cuba in 1960, Guillén continued to write and was made poet laureate and cultural ambassador of the Revolution by Castro.

CUBAN NOVELISTS

The sociologist, ethnologist and researcher into Cuba's musical past, Fernando Ortíz (1881–1969), enjoys a wide readership – and not just in the academic world. Historical novelist, Alejo Carpentier (1904–80), who was once a prisoner of the Machado regime and later Cuban consul in Paris, achieved fame outside Cuba.

Probably the most important representatives of the recent Cuban novel are Miguel Barnet (b.1940) and Reinaldo Arenas (1943–90). Jesús Díaz (b. 1941), who vehemently criticises conditions in Cuba, has incurred the wrath of Fidel Castro and, like all other literary figures opposed to his government, he lives in exile. Another Cuban exile is Guillermo Cabrera Infante (b.1929), whose novel *Three Trapped Tigers* (1971), about Havana's nightlife in the late 1950s, won international acclaim, and changed the course of Latin American fiction.

Below: José Martí
Bottom: Sloppy Joe's, a hub of Havana's nightlife in the 1950s

Music

What makes Cuban music so fascinating are its unique rhythms. Rumba, mambo and cha-chachá, all Cuban in origin, became dance crazes throughout the US and Europe in the first part of the 20th century, and salsa (literally sauce), a newer direction in Latin American music, also has its roots in Cuba. Most contemporary Cuban music is based on *son*, a fusion of African and Hispanic music. Originally, a lead singer with two backing singers who played the maracas – gourd rattles inherited from pre-Hispanic times – were accompanied by a *tres*, a type of guitar with three double strings, and a pair of small hand drums gripped between the knees. Later, more percussion instruments, such as the congas, timbales *campanas* (cowbells), were added.

Below: playing the congas
Bottom: rhythm band

RHYTHM BANDS

A traditional Cuban rhythm band consists of three musicians: a *bongocero*, a drummer who maintains a 'hammering' beat called a *martillo*, improvising with the singers and occasionally changing to the *campana*; the *conguero*, who provides a basic background rhythm, e.g. with the *tumbao*, and also plays solo; and the *timbalero* who varies the main rhythm using drums and a

wooden block. *Claves*, two short wooden sticks tapped together to set the beat, are perhaps the most important element in Cuban music and give the rhythmic base for *son* and rumba. One of Cuba's oldest bands, Los Van Van, developed the popular salsa dance music. And renowned band Irakere has merged Cuban rhythms with jazz.

AFRICAN SOURCES

The forefathers of black Cubans came from the Yoruba region of what is now Nigeria and Benin and many other areas of Africa: both West Africa and Central Bantú-speaking regions (Congo, Angola, etc). All African groups brought with them their own percussive heritage. Yoruba groups were one of the most influential and Santería is based around Yoruba beliefs. For them, song, dance and drums were closely linked with their belief in the *orishas* (deities), and the Yoruba devised at least one rhythm for each deity. The Cubans draw their inspiration from these rhythms performed on *batá* drums *(see right)*. To the untutored ear, the complex rhythms may seem like a wild cacophony, but they are actually highly structured and complex. Many of the rhythms associated with music such as Swing, Funk and Rap owe their origins to Afro-Cuban drummers.

Santería

From an air-conditioned glass niche on the first floor of the pilgrims' church in El Cobre *(see page 79)*, a statue of the Virgen de la Caridad (Virgin of Charity) in a splendid, golden costume looks down at the altar. Candles releasing the scent of myrrh burn at the foot of the national saint.

However, it is impossible to say how many of those kneeling in front of the figure are praying to the Roman Catholic Madonna and how many are seeking succour from Ochún, the African goddess of love, flowers and rivers, and one of Santería's principal *orishas* (deities). The sea of yellow flowers and glasses full of water point with some certainty to the intentions of her followers,

Batá rhythms
Resting on the thighs of the drummer, *batá* drums are played by hand by three musicians in the ensemble. The largest *batá*, called the *iya*, sets the tone and carries one rhythm forward into the next. The *itotele*, the middle-sized drum, keeps up a basic rhythm and answers the 'calls' of the *iya*, while the smaller *okonkolo* introduces an additional basic rhythm against the *itotele*.

Below: feel the rhythm
Bottom: flowers for Ochún

Personal gods

What makes the *orishas*, or gods, so appealing is that they have both divine and human characteristics, and are part of the family. Everyone has their own patron saint, their *santo*, who is always at their side when problems arise. As a symbol of their closeness, believers wear a bracelet or necklace in their god's favourite colour. Everyday items are usually used for the rituals: porcelain or clay figures represent the gods, and special sacred essences are kept in soup terrines and then locked in the cupboard with glasses full of water for the spirits of the dead.

indicating that belief in Santería is stronger in Cuba than in the Roman Catholic faith. There are at least another 20 Afro-Cuban *orishas*, apart from Ochún. Changó, for example, is Ochún's husband, the god of virility and war. He combines many human strengths and weaknesses, such as hard work, courage, deceit and boastfulness. His Roman Catholic counterpart is St Barbara. Obatalá, the androgynous son of Olofí, the father of the gods, is regarded as the creator of the human race and the god of peace, and is often associated with Jesus or Nuestra Señora de la Merced.

These African gods arrived in Cuba with the slaves, who, despite a forced baptism, continued to worship them in secret. Gradually, the two beliefs became entwined – saints and spirits merged under the mantle of Catholicism.

The rites of Santería are controlled by a *babalawo*, a priest who mediates between man and spirit for the most complex and important divinations. He is responsible for conducting the ceremonies and is also a kind of soothsayer. During a ceremony, he dances to the beat of the drum to summon the spirits to earth, so that they find refuge in the body of the *santero* and speak directly to him, thus inducing a trance-like state. Every deity has their own drumbeat, song, dance and colour; they also have preferred foods and drinks, perhaps *aguardiente de caña* (sugar cane

Santería dancers

rum). To predict the future, the *babalawo* throws shells, bones and pieces of coconut on the ground and then draws conclusions from the positions they have landed in.

Festivals and Events

Carnival has always been an important time of year for Cubans. It is the time when the African roots of many of the islanders are at their most conspicuous. Suspended in 1992 due to cash shortages, the Carnival is now back on the agenda. Santiago de Cuba holds the most spectacular festival around the end of July to mark the *zafra* or the end of the sugar cane harvest. For several weeks, night and day, the streets pulsate with a riot of colour and movement. Havana has smaller ones throughout the year, and Varadero puts one on in January or February. The people are also encouraged to celebrate national events when official parades are often followed by smaller gatherings in the localities.

Below and bottom: performers at La Mina in Havana

1 January: Liberation Day
January/February: Carnival (in Varadero and Havana)
28 January: José Martí's birthday
February: Festival to mark the end of the pineapple harvest on the Isla de la Juventud
April: Festival del Caribe in Santiago de Cuba
1 May: Labour Day
June: Cucalambé folk festival in Las Tunas; Festival de Cultura Caribena in Santiago de Cuba
21–27 July: Sugar cane harvest carnival (in Santiago); Santiago's Carnival
26 July: Anniversary of the attack on Moncada Barracks
10 October: Beginning of the First War of Independence
October/November: International Ballet Festival in Havana with related events in the regions
16 November: San Cristóbal Day, Havana's patron saint
December: International Latin American Film Festival in Havana
25 December: Christmas

FOOD AND DRINK

CROCODILE TAIL AND COCONUT

A cynical traveller once noted that Cuba is like the final courses of a fine evening's dining: there is plenty of coffee, ample sugar and a marvellous Havana. This observation highlights, perhaps unkindly but accurately, the problems that the Cuban government is facing when it comes to supplying its population with adequate amounts of food.

The food that is served up to ordinary Cubans every day is meagre and plain. Don't expect haute cuisine. Until 1989 anyone who had a right to a *libreta* (ration book) could claim a weekly ration of chicken and ice-cream. But since then, because of the shortages, the Government has had to cut back on the nation's diet. Minced meat quotas are supplemented with soya, bread dough with sweet potato flour, coffee with ground peas, while tinned milk is used as a milk substitute for babies.

But not all is doom and gloom. Since self-employment was legalised, the food that is available has improved. It is also better (and cheaper) in *paladares* – a few tables in somebody's home – and the best food is usually to be found in the *casa particulares*, although only guests may eat there. In addition, traditional snacks have reappeared on the street.

On the menu in the luxury hotels are dishes which the average Cuban can only dream about. The chefs know the sort of thing that the tourists and foreign businessmen and women enjoy. Usually there will be a creation with a creole *(criolla)* flavour. You will be confronted with plenty of buffets, usually better in the internationally-run hotels than Cuban ones.

Crocodile tail and coconut are two delicacies not to be found in hotels.

Refreshing coconut milk can be bought from the *ranchos* or *ranchones*. These rustic-style, straw-covered bar-restaurants are usually located near the main tourist sights, and occasionally by the main roads.

Crocodile meat is a speciality only available in the crocodile farm area of La Boca and Guaná *(see page 59)* on the south coast. Roasted until crispy, it tastes rather like chicken.

American-style fast food has recently arrived in Cuba. Stalls have sprung up by the roadside in the tourist resorts, selling lemonade, hamburgers, sandwiches and *churros* (deep-fried sugared doughnut sticks). El Rapido is a fast food chain found in various parts of the country. Pizza is very popular in restaurants and on the street.

MOORS AND CHRISTIANS

Cuba's cuisine contains a mixture of African, Caribbean and Hispanic influences. The most popular accompaniment to meat is *moros y cristianos* (Moors and Christians) consisting of white rice with black beans, but *congrí* or rice with kidney beans is another favourite. Potatoes are rarely served unless they are sweet, though purée is popular when available.

Improvisations

Due to the economic difficulties of the last decade, cooks have had to improvise with what ingredients are available. Spices, traditional in Cuban cuisine, have been substituted with lemon peel, dried avocado and celery leaves; *sofrito*, a paste of onion, garlic, pepper and oil, is often replaced by *mojo*, a mixture of lime, garlic and oil; meat stews are plumped out with vegetables.

Plátano or plantain, which looks like a large banana, is used a lot in cooking and is very versatile, eaten ripe or green, fried or boiled, but never raw. It may be considered a lowly ingredient but it is very filling

A typical breakfast consists of fruit, eggs and coffee. A fruit salad, usually with grapefruit, orange, sometimes pineapple and banana, is often served as a creole-style hors d'oeuvre. Pawpaws, mangoes, avocados and melons are sometimes available, but servings are unlikely to be generous.

CHICKEN OR PORK

For the main meal, starters usually comprise a fresh salad made from white cabbage, cucumber, tomato and sometimes *palmito* (palm heart). The main-course choice is usually between chicken or pork: probably *pollo asado* (roast chicken) or *cerdo asado* (roast pork). Beef, although uncommon, is served in thin, hard slices or in a goulash *(picadillo)*. These will be accompanied by root vegetables such as *malanga, boniato* (sweet potato), *yuca* (cassava) or *ñame* (yam) known collectively as *vianda* – all delicious but rather filling. It is unusual to find vegetables served raw or even lightly cooked.

Surprisingly, fish is not a part of the everyday diet, as it is regarded by Cubans as something only the poor eat, so the locals do not complain that fish and seafood is being pushed as a potential export. It is illegal for Cubans to eat lobster or to offer lobster and prawns *(camarones)* to tourists in *paladares*, but some people risk the huge fines and offer them all the same. If you are offered lobster, be discreet about it.

As well as fruit salad, the dessert menu (if one is available) will list crème caramel *(flan)*, brought to Cuba by the Spanish settlers, glacé pawpaws with a pastry called *buñuelos*, made from *yuca* and *boniato*, or perhaps guava marmalade with cheese *(guayaba con queso)*. A strong, black coffee with plenty of sugar known as *café mezclado* rounds off the meal.

Light snacks include *pan con lechón* (bread roll with suckling pig), *bocadito con cerdo* (bread roll with pork), *tamales* (maize flour pockets with meat) or *palitroque* (bread sticks). A traditional lunchtime snack is the humble *bocadillo con jamón y queso* (ham and cheese sandwich).

COCKTAILS AND SUNDOWNERS

To make a *mojito*, three-year-old white rum, lime juice, sugar and soda are mixed together with ice and then flavoured with *yerba buena*, a type of mint. *Daiquirí* is an iced drink containing rum, lime juice, and syrup or sugar. *Cuba libre*, literally 'free Cuba', gets its name from the nationalist Cuban slogan of the Wars of Independence and was, it is said, invented by American troops in 1898. This mixture of cola and rum, cola for America and rum for Cuba, is still widely available. Cubans love beer: Bucanero and Cristal are the most common, but other brands such as Tínima (from Camagüey) and Mayabe (from Holguín) are also very good. Imported beers from Europe and Canada are also easy to find.

> **Hemingway's favourite tipple**
> Ernest Hemingway used to enjoy a midday *mojito* in La Bodeguita del Medio bar. For his evening *daiquiris*, he frequented El Floridita, where a bar stool was reserved for him and where you'll now find a lifesize bronze statue of the writer, propped up against the bar. His remark '*Mi mojito en La Bodeguita y mi daiquirí en El Floridita*' may have brought plenty of business to his two favourite bars in Old Havana, but his passion for Cuban cocktails left the convivial novelist with a serious dose of liver cirrhosis.

RUM

It all began in a wooden barn in Santiago during 1838 when Spanish immigrant Facundo Bacardí decided to try and improve the local rum. He managed to obtain a cast-iron still and started experimenting, eventually coming up with his so-called 'light rum'. Bacardí's small distillery developed into a thriving factory, which he later moved to Havana. After the Revolution, the factory was nationalised and the Bacardí family fled to Puerto Rico. The rum continued to be made in Havana under the name Havana Club and in Santiago under the name of Santiago de Cuba and Caney. The nationalised Caney factory in Santiago *(see page 75)*, where currently 250 people are employed (70 percent are women), produces 9 million litres of rum each year. About 60 percent of this is for the export market, 20 percent is taken home by tourists and 20 percent is drunk locally.

Although Havana Club is still the most popular rum in the hotel bars, many Cubans consider Matusalém to be better. Caney, Varadero and Caribbean Club are also well-known brands. Gran Reserva, a rum that is left to mature in barrels for 15 years, is the best and most expensive variety (about US$85 a bottle). Like whisky, the brown five- and seven-year-old rums (US$5–8) are drunk neat or with ice. The white three-year-old rum is mostly used in cocktails.

Restaurant Selection

The following are recommended restaurants for some of the most popular destinations described in this guide. They are listed according to three categories: $$$ = expensive; $$ moderate; $ = inexpensive.

The telephone network is in the process of being updated, so you may experience problems with some numbers. On the whole, it is not usually necessary to book unless you want to go to one of the very well-known restaurants such as La Bodeguita del Medio in Old Havana.

Havana

Las Ruinas, Parque Lenin, Calle 100 esq. a Cortina, tel: 07-578523. In the ruins of an old sugar factory. International menu. Famous and pricey. $$; **Restaurante 1830**, Malecón 1252 esq. a Calle 20, Vedado, tel: 07-553090. Grand restaurant serving international fare. $$$; **La Divina Pastora**, Complejo Turístico Morro-Cabaña, La Habana del Este, tel: 07-338341. Fish a speciality. Meals served on the terrace. $$; **La Mina**, Obispo 109 e/ Oficios y Mercaderes, La Habana Vieja, tel: 07-862 0216. Street café and restaurant, serving Cuban cuisine in an Andalusian atmosphere. Live music at lunchtime and in the evening. $$; **La Bodeguita del Medio**, Empedrado 207, La Habana Vieja, tel: 07-867 1374. Friendly bar with restaurant at the rear, once frequented by Ernest Hemingway. Sadly, the quality of food does not match its reputation. $$$; **El Floridita**, Monserrate 557 esq. Obispo, La Habana Vieja, tel: 07-631060. Bar in a modern, but rather sterile atmosphere. Hemingway drank the overpriced *daiquirís* here. $$$; **El Patio**, San Ignacio 54, Plaza de la Catedral, La Habana Vieja, tel: 07-867 1034. Cuban and international fare served on an idyllic patio or the balcony on the first floor, overlooking the square. Downstairs is known as El Patio, upstairs is called the **Paillada del Marqués**, tel: 867 1034 and is open until midnight. $$$.

Varadero

Mansión Xanadú, Ave de las Américas, tel: 045-667750. French-style international cuisine in the former Du Pont summer residence. Food does not quite match the atmosphere or the prices. Reservation recommended. **$$$**; **El Rancho**, Hotel Tuxpan, Ave de las Américas, tel: 045-667560. Creole fare in gourmet style. **$$$**; **El Bodegón Criollo**, 1ª Avenida esq. a Calle 40, tel: 045-667784. Sit outside on the covered terrace and enjoy tasty creole food. Open 24 hours. **$$**; **El Mesón del Quijote**, Ave de las Américas, La Torre, tel: 045-667796. Good Spanish food with appropriate music and fun, informal atmosphere. **$$**; **Café/Bar Mediterraneo**, Ave Primera esq. a Calle 40. Clean and friendly bar with a range of fast-food. **$**; **El Ranchoncita Criolla**, Ave Primera esq. a Calle 40. Creole snack bar under palm trees. By Varadero's lively main boulevard. **$**.

Las Terrazas/Soroa

Cafetal Buena Vista, Complejo Turístico Las Terrazas, Autopista Havana – Pinar del Río, 51km (32 miles), tel: 082-778555. Very good food served in restored 19th-century coffee plantation buildings. Excellent service to the accompaniment of *música campesina*. Open for lunch only, 11am–4pm. **$$**.

Pinar del Río

Rumayor, Ctra a Viñales, 1km (½ mile). Nothing spectacular, but the chef pulls out all the stops on his *pollo ahumado* (smoked chicken). **$**; **Viñales**, Casa de Don Tomás at C/. Salvador Cisneros 140, tel: 08-793 6300. Specialises in a mixed paella-like dish. Attractive wooden house, dating from the late 19th century. Open until 10pm.

Cienfuegos

Palacio de Valle, Ave 37, Punta Gorda, tel: 0432-551226. Dining out in a Moorish palace is a memorable experience, the sophisticated creole/ international fare, mainly seafood, a real delight. **$$$**; **Casa del Pescador**,

Ctra. Pasacaballo, 28km (17 miles), tel: 0432-48160. Regional seafood dishes served from 9am until 5pm. **$$**.

Trinidad

El Jiguë, Real esq. a Boca, tel: 0419-4315. Elegant restaurant in the heart of the Old Town on the tiny Plazuela del Jigüe. Creole dishes at reasonable prices. **$$**; **Mesón del Regidor**, Bolívar 424, tel: 0419-3756. Everything rustic, including the house, the tables and the tasty grilled dishes. **$$**; **Trinidad Colonial**, Maceo 402 esq. a Colón, tel: 0419-6473. In a lovely old colonial house with an inviting garden. Criollo cuisine (pork, chicken, fish, prawns). **$$**; **La Canchánchara**, Real 70, tel: 0419-4345. Sample such traditional drinks as *canchánchara* (aguardiente, lime juice, honey and ice) or *guarapo* (pressed sugar cane juice). **$**.

Santiago de Cuba

1900, San Basilio 354, tel: 0226-23507. Excellent creole cuisine served in lavish Art Nouveau ambience. Cuban peso restaurant. **$$$**; **El Bodegón**, Plaza Dolores e/ Valiente y María Rodriguez. Typical Cuban restaurant with bar, where tourists rarely stray. Excellent food accompanied by a friendly, relaxed atmosphere. **$$**; **Punta Gorda**, Ctra. de Punta Gorda, tel: 0226-91765. Fish and fresh lobsters served right beside Santiago Bay. Excellent reputation. Open: noon–10pm. **$$**; **El Mesón del Morro**, Ctra. del Morro, tel: 0226-91576. Pleasant terrace restaurant adjacent to the El Morro fortress serving very good creole food. Wonderful view across the bay. Open: 9am–9pm. **$$**; **Matamoros**, Calvario 508 e/ Aguilera y Enramada, tel: 0226-22675. Popular café and restaurant in the city centre by the Plaza de Dolores. Regular live music with guitar combos. **$$**; **El Cayo**, Cayo Granma in Santiago Bay, tel: 0226-41769. Excellent seafood served in a marine setting. **$$**; **Café Isabelica**, Plaza Dolores esq. Aguilera y Calvario. Probably the most attractive café in Cuba – and a good place to meet Cubans. Foreigners pay in dollars. **$**. **Don Antonio**, Plaza Dolores, tel: 0226-52307. Good creole food in an atmospheric beige stone colonial building. **$**.

Baconao National Park

Bocajagua, Parque Baconao. Daytrippers' restaurant in the park, near Playa del Indio. Mackerel with lime is the *tour de force*. **$$$**.

Manzanillo

El Golfo, 1 de Mayo y N. López, tel: 023-53158. A gastronomic experience for lovers of fish and seafood. Pay in Cuban pesos not dollars. **$$$**.

Bayamo

1513, García esq. a Lora, tel: 023-425921. Exceedingly good creole cooking. **$$**.

Guardalavaca

El Ancla, Playa Guardalavaca, Guardalavaca, tel: 024-30145. Seafood a speciality, but you could try the tasty creole pork with *yuca* and *boniato*. Arrive early because after 9pm you will go hungry. **$$**.

Isla de la Juventud

La Insula, C/. 39 esq. 22, tel: 321825. Reasonably-priced restaurant serving beef and lobster. Open until 10pm. **$$**; **El Cochinito**, Calle 39 esq. a 24, Gerona, tel: 046-322809. One of the better restaurants in the town, but the quality of the food is often rather mediocre. Pork a speciality. Open until 10pm. **$$**; **Casa de los Vinos**, Calle 20 esq. a 41, Gerona, tel: 046-324889. Fare revolves around sausages and local wines, unusual elsewhere on Cuba. Try *guachi*, a pineapple brandy. **$**.

Cayo Largo

El Criollo, Plaza Central, next to the Marina Puerto Sol. Very satisfying creole fare, but the bus stop in front makes it unpleasant outside. **$$**; **Taberna del Pirata**, Marina Puerto Sol. Fresh lobsters and fish – with creole music. **$$**.

Baracoa

El Castillito at Calixto García s/n, tel: 0121-45165. This place serves regional Baracoan cuisine; **Restaurant La Colonial** at Martí 123, tel: 0121-45391. An atmospheric *paladar* with good service and tasty food. Open until 11pm.

Lobster supper

NIGHTLIFE

Much of the nightlife in Cuba happens in the hotels. They all have bars and many provide entertainment which could be anything from salsa classes to discos and top-quality cabaret. To experience the local nightlife it's best to ask around for the top disco or cabaret in the neighbourhood. These are liveliest at the weekend and don't usually get going until 11pm or midnight. Although the resort of Varadero has the most prolific nightlife, Havana has the best.

Havana

Tropicana, Calle 72 No. 4505 e/ 41 y 45, Marianao, tel: 07-267 1717. Cuba's most celebrated cabaret. Extravagant dance shows on an open-air stage, starting at 10pm, admission from 9pm (by reservation only). **Ballet Nacional de Cuba**, Teatro Nacional, Paseo esq. a Calle 39, Vedado, tel: 07-879 6011. World-class dance performances such as *Swan Lake* and *Giselle* in the heart of the Caribbean. Reservation essential. **Disco Habana Club**, Hotel Comodoro, Calle 3 esq. a 84, Miramar. An estab-

Tropicana – Cuba's most celebrated cabaret

lished disco where they play music for an older crowd.

Santiago de Cuba

Tropicana, off Autopista Nacional km 1.5, tel: 0226-87090. Competition for Havana's Tropicana show, but much less touristy. Starts at 10pm. **Teatro José Heredia**, Ave de las Américas, tel: 0122-620510. Opened in 1991 with 2,500 seats, this is Cuba's largest theatre. Opera, concerts and ballet. Starts at 9pm. **Espantasueños**, Hotel Santiago de Cuba, tel: 0226-42656/687170 x374. Disco in town. Open: 9.30pm–3am.

Cayo Largo

Blue Lake, at the airport. The only disco away from the holiday complex, in the *bohío*-style arrival hall.

Varadero

Continental Cabaret, Hotel Internacional, Ctra de las Américas, tel: 045-667038. A small cabaret at an accessible price. **La Rumba**, Ave Las Américas km 4, tel: 045-668210 or **Mambo Club** on the Autopista Sur are both better. Both have an open bar for the $10 entrance fee. Open 10.30pm–3am.

ACTIVE HOLIDAYS

Waterskiing, sailing, snorkelling, diving, fishing, yachting, along with basketball, volleyball, squash, tennis and horse riding are available at many holiday centres, often with qualified instructors. An increasing number of hotels will also hire out bicycles and mopeds to guests.

Serious runners come for the marathons held on the island such as the one in Varadero in November.

DIVING AND SNORKELLING

Cuba's coral reefs, among the largest in the world, are a diver's paradise and they are never crowded. The coral grows at a depth of up to 400m (1,300ft) and even at 50m (164ft) the water is crystal clear. As opposed to many other Caribbean islands where over-exposure to tourism has destroyed some of the reefs, the coral here is alive and well and teeming with colourful fish.

Good, well marked areas for diving can be found all around the island. The waters off Isla de la Juventud have been established as a marine park and, with Cayo Largo and the Cayería del Norte on the Camagüey archipelago, are probably the most favoured spots. In many places, near Cayo Levisa for example, diving teams are exploring wrecks of sunken ships.

The main diving centres are members of CMAS (Confédération Mondiale de l'Activité Subaquatique) and groups are in the hands of expert guides. Diving schools exist in almost all the main coastal resorts and they can provide reliable equipment and lead weights, although often in limited numbers. Divers should bring their own mask and flippers if they have them, as these can be in short supply at some sites. Courses are run for beginners, and advanced divers are expected to produce their certification card, which should not be more than a year old, plus a log book. One diving trip costs about US$25–35, a carnet for 10 trips US$220–280.

The Cuban coral reefs are protected by law and it is strictly forbidden to hunt with harpoons and spears. It is also illegal to break off pieces of coral or remove shells from the water. Anyone found contravening the regulations will be banned from diving.

The **Hotel Colony**, Ensenada de la Siguanea, 41km (25 miles) southwest of Nueva Gerona, Isla de la Juventud, has some of Cuba's best scuba diving facilities, including a decompression chamber. Tel: 046-398181.

Hiking in the interior

Away from the cities, the countryside is rich in diverse landscapes — mountain ranges, rainforest, swampland and fertile valleys — just asking to be explored. Around 116 hiking trails and paths thread their way through scenery that is home to a wide array of tropical plants, birds and other creatures. Campsites *(see page 123)* are conveniently placed along some of the routes if you're up to making more than a day of it. Several regions have been designated by UNESCO as biosphere reserves. One of these is the Sierra del Rosario reserve, where from the eco-resort of Las Terrazas you can explore the surrounding forests with a guide *(see page 54)*. In the Sierra Maestro you can walk along trails to where the rebels once hid and fought during the wars of Independence and the Revolution. A two- to three-day trek includes climbing Cuba's highest peak, Pico Turquino *(see page 82)*, but only for the fit. Ask at your hotel for details. Also hikes in the Sierra del Escambray near Trinidad and in the Baracoa area.

FISHING

You do not have to have read Hemingway to imagine the pleasure that deep-sea anglers derive from catching a marlin out on the open sea. Most of the **deep-sea fishing** trips by yacht or motor boats last the whole day, but are not exclusively for angling enthusiasts, more for those who enjoy a challenge. The boats usually moor on an island at lunchtime and whatever the anglers have caught is cooked on the spot.

The atmosphere is very different during the fishing competitions that start out from the pleasure harbours, for example at Marina Hemingway in Havana. The deep-sea fishing season runs from May to December, with white marlin fishing competitions held almost monthly. For further information, contact **Tour & Travel**, C/. O y 21, Vedado, tel: 07-873 7109.

Freshwater reservoirs such as Zaza, near Sancti Spíritus, and La Redonda, provide excellent **flyfishing** and **angling**, with the large-mouth bass being the most popular catch. **Bonefishing** is popular off the archipelago of Los Jardines de la Reina to the south. For more information ask at the tourist information desk in your hotel.

Sailing at Cayo Levisa

SAILING AND WINDSURFING

The ever-present trade winds create the ideal conditions – and there is no need for a wetsuit either. Sailing and windsurfing centres where boats and boards can be hired are mainly to be found at the big hotels. One belongs to the **Hotel Internacional**, Ctra de las Américas, Varadero, tel: 045-63011, fax: 337246.

GOLF

As far as the Cuban government is concerned, golf is for capitalists. Nevertheless, there are two golf courses on the island: the **Havana Golf Club** in Havana (18 holes), Ctra de Vento, 8km (5 miles) from Reparto Capdevila, Ave Rancho Boyeros, tel: 07-558746; the other is in Varadero near the Mansión Xanadú, Ctra Las Américas km 8.5, tel: 045-667749. This is an 18-hole course and there are more planned for the area.

HORSE-RIDING

Horses can be hired in the main tourist centres. The pleasures of riding on horseback might not be appreciated in full, however, as the animals are not the liveliest of creatures. It is best to go riding in the early morning, when the horses are at their freshest and it is not so hot.

PRACTICAL INFORMATION

Getting There

BY AIR

Cubana de Avación (Cubana Airlines), the Cuban national airline, flies to Havana, Holguín, Santiago de Cuba, Cayo Largo, Camagüey and Varadero in Cuba from London (Gatwick), Paris, Geneva, Las Palmas, Lisbon, Moscow, Madrid, Barcelona, Santiago de Compostela, Rome and Milan. Charter flights are available from London, Vienna, Cologne, Paris, Frankfurt, Milan, Lisbon and Madrid.

The flying time from London to Havana is nine hours 40 minutes; 20 minutes shorter from Manchester.

Outside Europe, Cubana runs flights from Montreal in Canada and major cities in South America and Mexico, as well as Jamaica and Costa Rica: flights operate from Nassau in the Bahamas; Santo Domingo in the Dominican Republic; Guayaquil and Quito in Ecuador; Mexico City and Cancún in Mexico; Buenos Aires in Argentina; Montego Bay in Jamaica; Montevideo in Uruguay; and Santiago in Chile.

British travel agents voted Cubana the Worst Airline in 1999, due to an extremely bad customer service on the Cuban side; however it's still a cheap, quick and easy way of getting to Cuba.

Cubana Airlines, 49 Conduit Street, London WIR 9FB, tel: 020-7734 1165; fax: 020-7437 0681; Calle 23 #64, esq. Infanta y La Rampa, Vedado, Havana, tel: 07-334949.

Among other airlines serving Cuba are **Iberia** via Madrid and **Air France** via Paris, as well as **British Airways**, which commenced flights from London Gatwick in the spring of 1999. Charter flights include **Air UK** which flies direct to Camagüey from Gatwick; **Airtours** from Manchester to Varadero, and **Monarch Airlines** from Gatwick to Holguín, Varadero and Ciego de Avila. The Dutch charter airline **Martinair** flies from Amsterdam to Holguín and Varadero. **Air Canada** and **Royal Airlines** fly from Toronto to Varadero with charter flights from Ottawa.

Cuba has nine international airports, but most scheduled international flights arrive at Terminal 3 at Havana's **José Martí airport**, about 17km (10 miles) from the city centre, tel: 07-335177–79. If you are on a package holiday, a representative should meet you and organise your transfer from the airport to the hotel. Otherwise, the most efficient way to get to your destination is by taxi (US$12–18).

UK TOUR OPERATORS

More and more tour operators are including Cuba as a destination in their brochures, with many of them offering all-inclusive and tailor-made packages, such as weddings, sports, health or twin-centre holidays. The following are a small selection: **Airtours**, tel: 01706 240 033; **Captivating Cuba**, tel:020-8891 2222; **Ramblers Holidays**, tel: 01707 331 133; **Sun Modilex**, tel: 0870 242 4211.

> **Arriving by boat**
> People cruising on yachts in the Caribbean can stop off in Cuba at Marina Hemingway in Havana, or at marinas Gaviota, Chapelin, or Puertosol Dársena in Varadero, and at Cayo Largo, Maria La Gorda, Cienfuegos and Santiago. To enter the Cuban 12-mile zone, mariners should contact the port authorities on VHF channel 68 or SSB 2760 (national coastal network) or VHF 16 or SSB 2790 (tourism network).

Getting Around

It is difficult for independent travellers to make their own travel arrangements in Cuba. Using public transport can be a time-consuming business. Given the shortages of fuel and spare parts, bus journeys are restricted. There are no reliable timetables, but most travel agents such as **Havanatur** organise coach tours in vehicles that are usually comfortable and air-conditioned.

For further information contact: **Havanatur**, Edificio Sierra Maestra, Ave Ira. e/0 y 2, Miramar Playa, Havana, tel: 07-242056. This and other agents also have desks in tourist hotels.

BY ROAD
The Cuban roads are usually very quiet, but that is no reason to be any less careful when driving. Car indicators often do not work or are simply not used. Overtaking on the inside is common. In the cities watch out for cyclists. They dart across the traffic flow – usually without lights if it is dark – and represent a major hazard. In 1990 Castro imported a million or so bikes from China in order to get the country moving again. Further driving hazards include animals on the road and potholes, not to mention unmarked rail lines.

Cupet and **Oro Negro** petrol stations are provided for tourists, and these always have supplies of petrol, but you will have to pay in dollars. Most are open 24 hours a day. Try to keep the petrol tank at least half-full, as fuel stations are fairly thinly spread. Fuel stations accept credit cards, but sometimes the telephone lines are down so always have a cash reserve.

If you are travelling independently it is easy to get into difficulties, as road signs and signposts are few and far between. However, there is a new road atlas to Cuba (around US$12) which is a great bonus for drivers, a very sound investment.

Hitch-hiking is for Cubans only, local drivers may receive a huge fine if the police suspect them of running an illicit taxi service. However, during the day do pick up hitchers if you have your own vehicle.

Car Rental
The main international car rental companies do not have offices in Cuba, but local car rental firms, such as **Havanauto** or **Cubanacán**, do business in much the same way. The choice of vehicles is often very limited, and in high season you may want to consider booking in advance since they do go very quickly. Cars can be prone to breakdowns so make sure you are well insured beforehand.

Hotels have desks for at least one of these agents. You can also contact them at the airports: **Havanauto**, Aeropuerto José Martí, Havana, tel: 07-335197 or **Cubanacán**, Aeropuerto José Martí, Havana, tel: 07-333007.

By Taxi
Private taxis are a good way to get around Havana, but it is illegal for them, licensed or not, to ferry passengers to and from the airports. Always agree on the fare before starting your journey, as rates can vary quite dramatically between the different taxi companies. **Okay Taxi** are usually the dearest, followed by **Turistaxi**. **Cubataxi**, **Trans-Auto** and **Panataxi** (State-run) are usually cheaper.

BY AIR
Most internal flights are operated by **Cubana de Avación** (Cubana Airlines) which uses mainly smaller Antonovs and Yakolevs, as well as **AeroCaribbean**. Along with the provincial capitals, flights also serve

the following towns: Baracoa, Manzanillo, Nueva Gerona and Varadero. Internal flights from Havana use Terminal 1. Domestic flights are cheaper when booked in conjunction with an international flight on Cubana. Once in Cuba you can often book through your hotel or a local travel agency. Reserve as far in advance as possible if you want to be sure of a seat.

For further information, contact your hotel desk or **Cubana de Avación** *(see page 115)* and **Aero-Caribbean**, Calle 23 #64, Vedado, Havana, tel: 07-797524.

BY TRAIN

All trains tend to be very crowded, slow and prone to breakdown. Services have been reduced considerably since 1990 and most trains now stop at every station. Seats have to be booked well in advance as there are long waiting lists. However, there are always some reserved for those paying in dollars – usually a whole car. Tickets are available for dollar-paying passengers through **LADIS** (still often known by its old name of 'Ferrotur') inside the station or nearby.

BY BUS

Travel by local bus *(guaguas)* is only for the patient and hardy. For dollar-carrying visitors, tour buses *(see page 116)* are a more efficient and comfortable option. All hotels can book reasonably priced excursions to the main tourist destinations.

Facts for the Visitor

VISAS

All travellers to Cuba should be in possession of a passport which is valid for at least another six months at time of arrival, a return ticket and a tourist card *(tarjeta de turista)*. These are supplied by the travel agency, if you are on a package holiday. Independent travellers can purchase them at a cost of US$25 (£15) from the airline that sells them their ticket. If you are going it alone, you will also need a state hotel voucher on arrival for at least three overnight stays. Business people and journalists must apply for a business visa – contact your local Cuban consulate for details *(see page 121)*.

CUSTOMS

As well as their own personal belongings, which includes fishing gear and photographic equipment, visitors to Cuba can bring into the country two bottle of liquor, one carton of cigarettes and up to 10 kg (22lb) of medicines. Imported goods up the value of US$250 are taxed at 100 percent for four-fifths of their worth. Unlimited sums of money can be brought in but it's advisable to declare any amounts over US$5,000 – in order to take that amount back out, an appropriate customs declaration must be made.

EU citizens are not subject to any duties for souvenirs. The following duty-free restrictions do, however, apply when returning home: 200 cigarettes or 100 cigarillos or 50 cigars or 250g loose tobacco; 1 litre rum (above 22 percent alcohol) or 2 litres wines and spirits below 22 percent alcohol; 500g coffee.

Street names

After 1959 many street names were changed. In order to make it easier for visitors to find their way around, the point where two streets intersect is included in the address. So the address for the bar El Floridita in Havana is Calle Monserrate 557 esq. a Calle Obispo. In other words it is located at 557 Monserrate Street on the corner with Obispo Street. E/ in an address stands for *entre* (between). Often the word for street, *calle*, is omitted.

Under the CITES agreement, it is illegal to take home products such as crocodile skins, turtle shells and black coral, so make sure you know what you are buying when shopping.

TOURIST INFORMATION

In the UK: 167 High Holborn, London WC1V 6PA, tel: 020-7240 6655; e-mail: cubatouristboard.london@ virgin.net

In Canada: 55 Queen Street East, Suite 705, Toronto M5C 1R6, tel: 416-362 0700/2; e-mail: cuba.tbtor@sympatico.ca

In Cuba: All hotels and airports have a tourist information desk for general enquiries. There are several companies devoted to tourism such as **Infotur**, which can be found in **Havana** at Calle Obispo 358 e Habana y Compostela, tel: 07-333333, daily 8am–8pm, and in **Santiago de Cuba** at Ave Las Américas y M, tel: 0226-7278; in **Varadero** information can be obtained from **Havanatur**, Ave. Playa 3606, e/Calle 36 y Calle 37, tel: 045-63713.

Websites: www.cubaweb.cu (official Government site); www.cubatravel.com (tourist board).

CURRENCY AND EXCHANGE

The national currency is the Cuban peso (CUP), but visitors will need US dollars (called *dolares* or *divisa* in Cuba) as anything connected with tourism, e.g. hotels, souvenirs, museums etc., is charged in dollars. Keep a supply of small denominations, as even changing a US$20 note can cause problems. In local shops, prices in pesos are written with the dollar sign ($). It's a good idea to have a supply of Cuban pesos (commonly referred to as *moneda nacional*), for shopping from street vendors or at markets.

Credit cards are accepted at the airport, at car hire offices, travel agencies and in the larger tourist hotels and

Buying cigars

Cigars *(puros* or *habanos)* are available from street traders, but visitors should take care even when buying cheap goods. The cigars may carry reputable labels such as Cohibas, Monte Cristos or Romeo y Julietas, but they are likely to be fakes. You can only be sure of buying genuine cigars in the cigar factories, such as Partagás in Havana *(see page 38)*, or reputable cigar shops, often found in hotels, where you will be given two copies of an official stamped receipt one of which is to be given to customs on departure.

restaurants. Nowhere will accept American Express or any other card or travellers' cheques issued by an American bank e.g. Citibank.

Cash withdrawals can be made with a credit card in Havana, Varadero and some other cities of up to US$1,000, but you may be given convertible pesos (*pesos convertibles* in Spanish), in change. These notes and coins have been introduced by the Government to overcome the shortage of dollar notes and coins in circulation; they are fully interchangeable with the real thing but you must change them before you leave as they are worthless outside the country.

Banks and hotels change cash and travellers' cheques, but charge a commission of up to 4 percent. You can change dollars into Cuban pesos officially at exchange bureaux called CADECAS where you get a better rate and also give cash withdrawals on credit cards.

AIRPORT TAXES

Nobody can check in upon departure until a US$25 fee has been paid for the disembarkation tax.

OPENING TIMES

Shops open Monday to Saturday from

9.30am–12.30pm and 2–5pm, banks and post offices from 8.30am–noon and 1.30–3pm, but exceptions are common. Every second Saturday is a non-working day. Museums generally open from 9am–6pm, but tend to close at noon on Sunday. However, you cannot rely on these times. For example, some museums close early if they're getting few visitors that day.

SHOPPING
The supply of basic commodities continues to be a problem, although it has improved enormously of late. All the larger hotels have *tiendas*, where it is possible to buy a map or a souvenir. Dollar shops, such as **Diplotienda**, **Tecnitiendas**, *tiendas de artesanía* (craft shops) and **Intur** outlets are open only to those with dollars.

Souvenirs such as wood carvings or jewellery are often sold on street corners, but again it is a case of buyer beware. They may be made from hardwoods, black coral, polymita snail shells or turtle shell, materials which under the CITES agreement on the trade in protected wildlife cannot be exported.

SHOPPING OUTLETS
Diplotienda (Centro Comercial), 5ta Ave esq. a 42, Miramar, tel: 07-204 7070. Cuba's largest supermarket. Practically every luxury item is available here, and it is now open to Cubans as well. But it is expensive.

Palacio de la Artesanía, Cuba 64 y Tacón, La Habana Vieja, tel: 07-866 8072. An array of souvenir shops, selling musical instruments, Cuban and Caribbean music and cigars.

La Internacional, Obispo esq. a Bernaza, La Habana Vieja, tel: 07-861 3283. Large selection of books for dollars only, but attached to it is an excellent secondhand bookshop selling an interesting mixture for pesos.

Galería Victor Manuel, San Ignacio 56, Plaza de la Catedral, tel: 07-861 2955. Cuban paintings and handicrafts for sale.

Casa del Tabaco, Mercaderes 120 e/ Obispo y Obrapía, La Habana Vieja. Cigars and a tobacco museum.

Casa del Café, Obispo y Baratillo 51, La Habana Vieja. Cuban coffee – to drink or to take home.

Casa del Ron, Obispo esq. a Bernaza, La Habana Vieja, tel: 07-867 0817. Tobacco and drinks, with the speciality being rum.

TIPPING
Tipping in US dollars is very welcome –

Tempting trinkets

in fact for many families, the *propina* (tip) provides the main family income, and visitors should remember how important their dollars are to the local economy. Give US$1 to porters, waiters and other helpful individuals; for higher bills in restaurants US$2. Room maids appreciate about US$3 per week; they will also be glad of any unwanted clothes that you have. Give tour guides US$1 per member of the party per day. It's a good idea to bring with you sweets and pens which you can hand out to local children.

TIME
Cuba is five hours behind GMT, and is the equivalent of Eastern Standard Time in the United States and Canada. Clocks are turned back at the beginning of October and then forward towards the end of March.

VOLTAGE
If you are taking a hair dryer or electric shaver, then you will also need an adapter for 110V/60 Hz. Even in five-star hotels, hair dryers are not supplied as standard. You'll also find 220V in some places (e.g. big international hotels). Plugs are two flat pins.

POSTAL SERVICES
Stamps for postcards and letters cost about 75 cents. They can be obtained at hotels and post offices. It may take up to eight weeks for a letter to reach Europe via Spain, although a fortnight is normal.

TELEPHONE
It is possible to make calls either directly or via the *operador* from most large hotels. To call the US direct, dial 119-1; through the operator 661212.

To ring the UK, first dial 119, then the international code 44. A minute to the USA costs US$2; US$4.40 for most of the rest of the world. However,

you can make a local call for as little as US$0.05 in local money – a fraction of 1 US cent. Cards *(tarjetas)* from US$10 to US$45 are available from hotels. As everywhere else in the world it is more expensive to phone from a hotel. To phone Cuba from the UK dial 0053 before the number, 01153 from the USA.

The telephone exchanges have been undergoing vast reorganisation, which means telephone numbers in remote areas cannot always be reliable. Ask at tourist information desks if you have any difficulties getting through, (Spanish-only) directory enquiries is free: dial 113.

NEWSPAPERS AND MAGAZINES
Foreign newspapers never find their way into Cuba. However, in hotels you will find magazines from *Cosmopolitan* to *Time*. The only daily newspaper is *Granma*, the official organ of the Cuban Communist Party.

A serious shortage of paper accounts for the problems with supply and size. *Granma Internacional* is published every week in English. *Opciones* is a new, well-produced weekly focusing on the economy, finance and tourism, and may well be of interest to business people and holidaymakers. *Cartelera* appears at irregular intervals in English with information about events of interest to visitors; other tourist publications are sold in hotels and airports.

TV AND RADIO
In many hotels, the radios simply do not work or are set to just three or four stations. Several, including Radio Rebelde, broadcast to 1.6 million households with a diet of culture, music, quiz games and boxing contests. Radio Taíno on 93.3FM is a lively music station. Radio Reloj (Clock Radio) provides round-the-

clock news on AM backed by the irritating ticking of a loud clock.

Hotel rooms are usually equipped with televisions. In the large hotels, satellite dishes receive CNN and other stations. Clave Cubano is a Cuban-music version of MTV. Canal del Sol broadcasts information for tourists.

LANGUAGE

A little Spanish will prove very useful. Many younger people are now learning English and you may find yourself being approached by language students wishing to try out their language skills on you.

PHOTOGRAPHY

Apart from military installations, there are no limits on what visitors may photograph. Cubans are usually very happy to be included in holiday snaps. Colour film for normal and video cameras is available in many hotel and tourist shops, but the quality of developing is poor. Slide film is hard to come by and even harder to develop. The best time to take colour photos is 9.30–11.30am and after 4pm.

BATHING

The rules for swimming in the sea are as follows: a red flag means bathing is forbidden, yellow means caution and green all clear. It is advisable to wear sandals to protect against sea urchins. A strong sunblock and an effective insect repellent are essential.

NUDE BATHING

Brief bikinis and topless bathing are not usually acceptable, except in Varadero. Nude bathing is forbidden.

MEDICAL

Medical provision is available all over the island and the level of care is way above that of any other Caribbean country. However, given the shortage of medications, it is important to take any prescribed pills or ointments with you. Emergency treatment is free, but follow-on and other treatments and medications must be paid for in dollars which are not cheap.

INSURANCE

Insurance against cancellation, accident, illness and theft is essential.

INOCULATIONS

No inoculations are offically required by the Cuban immigration authorities unless you are arriving from an area where cholera, smallpox or yellow fever exists. However, it is advisable for your own peace of mind to be immunised against Hepatitis A and typhoid.

DRINKING WATER

Never drink tap water.

DISABLED

Discrimination of any kind is prohibited in Cuba. Cubans are always willing to help disabled people. However, there is little in the way of 'infrastructure' for disabled people and hotels only have a very limited number of rooms – if any – that are properly equipped, so book in advance.

CRIME

Since the Revolution, theft has been regarded as a serious offence. Anyone caught stealing would be pursued by crowds of people, handed over to the police and punished. However, in recent years, the crime rate has increased dramatically.

DIPLOMATIC REPRESENTATION

Great Britain: Calle 34 #708 Miramar, Havana, tel: 07-241771. **Canada**: Calle 30 #518 esq. a 7ma, Miramar, tel: 07-332516. **United States** (Interests Section): Calzada e/ L y M, Vedado, tel: 07-333551–9.

ACCOMMODATION

Since the Communist Party turned to tourism as its saviour, it has been treated like a rare plant. The grand colonial-style hotels have been spruced up, other decaying establishments renovated and new ones built with all the latest facilities.

In 1994, the tourist industry was reorganised and a company called **Cubanacán SA** was founded in order to bring tourism under State control. Each area of activity, such as hotel accommodation, restaurants, entertainment and souvenir shops, has been formed into a separate organisation. So, the **Gran Caribe** group is responsible for luxury hotels, **Horizontes** for three-star hotels, and **Islazul** for one- and two-star hotels. However, it is worth noting that the Cuban star categories do not necessarily correspond with European ratings.

Since then hotels have been mushrooming all over the country: 22 four-star hotels opened for business in 2000 alone, and more are in the pipeline. The Government has also been encouraging the self-catering holiday market, and new grocery shops have opened up here and there to sell provisions.

Access to hotels is via a tourist card and a colourful plastic bracelet. Guests use the card to gain entry to their restaurant and as a voucher for meals, and may be asked at any time to produce it, so it serves as a sort of passport. Official passports may therefore be left in the hotel.

A DIFFERENT CUBA

When you enter a hotel, you become part of a world that is alien to most Cubans. The usual amenities that globe-trotting tourists expect, such as restaurants, bars, souvenir shops, travel agents and car rental offices, are available as standard. Many hotels also have a swimming pool, fitness centre, disco, cabaret and emergency medical post.

A special distribution network keeps tourist areas well supplied, so visitors do not often encounter the sort of shortages that the locals have to constantly put up with; but when the island's supplies of light bulbs or paper towels run out, then the luxury hotels have the same problem. At times, the electricity can be cut off for hours. All rooms are equipped as double rooms. Reductions of 20 to 25 percent apply to single occupancies.

Do not set your sights too high in hotels away from the main tourist centres of Varadero, Cayo Largo and Havana. Cuban hosts try hard to please their guests but, as staff have little idea of standards abroad, it is not always easy to meet expectations.

Villas or *cabañas* are usually clustered around central amenities, such as the swimming pool, restaurant, bar or nightclub which belong to the adjoining hotel.

Camping is undoubtedly the cheapest way of holidaying and the sites are often situated in attractive spots, but the accommodation offered is not what Europeans understand by camping. Cabins, not unlike army barracks, are usually made of timber or prefabricated concrete. For more information, contact the **Cubamar** organisation. It's important to book in advance.

Grupo Cubanacán provide information about their hotels. Contact them at Cubanacán Skylines, Unit 49, Limeharbour, Docklands, London E14 9TS, tel: 020-7537 7909; fax: 020-7537 7747. **Horizontes** has a website: www.horizontes.cu

Hotel Selection

The following are suggestions for the most popular destinations described in this guide. They are listed according to three categories: **$$$** = expensive; **$$** = moderate; **$** = inexpensive. The telephone exchanges have been undergoing major reorganisation so you may still experience difficulty with some numbers in remoter areas.

Havana

Hotel Nacional de Cuba, Calle 0 esq. a 21, Vedado, tel: 07-855 0294; fax: 873 5171. Renovated luxury 1930s hotel. View of the sea and the Malecón. Magnificent garden. **$$$**; **Hotel Santa**

Casas Particulares

Staying in a room in someone's private house *(casa particular)* is a wonderful way of experiencing the real Cuba – and it's not expensive. Accommodation can range from a basic room to a luxury apartment, and may include breakfast and other meals, so you should check first. Until 1996 it was illegal for a Cuban to rent out rooms to tourists, but it was widely practised all the same. However, the rules that were imposed with legalisation, including high taxes, have been so restricting that some of the early *casas* have stopped 'trading'. Rooms cost US$15–35 per night

There is no central booking agency for *casas particulares*, so to find one you need to ask around: restaurant staff, taxi drivers, or fellow travellers can usually help, or you may be approached on the street by agents.

Independent visitors travelling on a tourist card are supposed to book into a State hotel for their first night in Cuba, which will allow some time for finding the right place. Proof of this is often asked for at Cuban Consulates when issuing your tourist card and you're expected to put down an address when arriving at immigration.

Isabel, Baratillo 9 e/ Obispo y Narciso López, Old Havana, tel: 07-860 8201; fax: 860 8391. Exquisite five-star right by the Plaza de Armas. **$$$**; **Meliá Cohiba**, Paseo e/ Calle 1 y 3, Vedado, tel: 07-333636; fax: 334555. Luxurious Spanish-run premises, opened on the seafront in 1995. One of the largest hotels in Cuba. **$$$**; **Plaza**, Agramonte 267, Parque Central, tel: 07-860 8583; fax: 860 8591. Elegant establishment with long tradition. **$$$**; **Sevilla**, Trocadero 55 e/ Zulueta y Prado, Centro Habana, tel: 07-860 8560; fax: 860 8582. Splendid hotel in Mudéjar style with 192 renovated rooms. **$$$**; **Inglaterra**, Paseo del Prado 416 esq. San Rafael, La Habana Vieja, tel: 07-608595/627072; fax: 608254. Renovated in 1993, this grand hotel dates from 1875 and is the oldest in Cuba. Open-air disco on the roof. **$$**; **Caribbean**, Paseo del Prado 164, tel: 07-860 8210. Basic hotel, close to La Habana Vieja. **$**; **Hostal Valencia**, Oficios 53 e/ Lamparilla y Obrapía, La Habana Vieja, tel: 07-571037. Small, striking building dating from the end of the 18th century. **$**.

Playas del Este

Villas Cuba, Ave Las Terrazas Sur y Calle 5a, Santa María del Mar, tel: 07-219198. Comfortable apartment hotel with nightclub. **$$$**; **Itabo**, Laguna Itabo, Santa María del Mar, tel: 0687-25889. In green surroundings only 150 metres (160yds) from the beach. **$$**; **Tropicoco Beach**, Ave. Sur y Las Terrazas, Santa María del Mar, tel: 687-2531. Hotel with disco and tennis courts, near the beach. **$$**.

Varadero

Meliá Las Américas, Autopista Sur, tel: 045-667600; fax: 045-667012. First-class establishment half-way along the Hicacos peninsula, beside a small, sandy bay, near the Du Pont mansion (Xanadú). **$$$**; **Iberostar Bella Costa**, Ave de las Américas, tel: 045-667210; fax: 667205. Luxurious five-storey complex under Spanish management, complete with a presidential suite. Ask for a room away from the generator. **$$$**; **Paradisus Varadero**, off the Autopista Sur, Varadero Beach, tel: 045-668700; fax: 668705. Opened in 2000 with 421 rooms, nine bars and restaurants, a gym and sauna; located in the area of the Reserva Ecológica Varahicacos. It's the most luxurious place on the peninsula – an exclusive all-inclusive resort. Suba diving is included. **$$$**; **Sol Palmeras**, Ctra las Morlas, tel: 045-667009. Quiet palm garden and Spanish/ Caribbean architecture. Family-friendly. **$$**; **Internacional**, Ctra de las Américas, tel: 045-667038; fax:

Health farms in the tropics

Health, anti-stress and 'quality of life' holidays are very popular in Cuba, where well-equipped spa hotels with fully qualified staff offer a multitude of programmes and therapeutic treatments in beautiful settings. Cuba has many mineral springs, and medicinal research is being carried out on around 30 of them. The Government started promoting health tourism in the 1980s to boost the economy, and foreigners were invited over for a face lift, heart bypass, or other medical procedure at a low cost. Now, combined with pleasure tourism, the health market is taking off, and there are many well-equipped centres available for dollars. Defying the old adage that health and fun don't mix, nightlife, sightseeing, sport and nature can be woven into programmes catering for all types of problems, from orthopaedic and neurological to improving your quality of life. Horizontes and Cubanacán *(see page 123)* run spa hotels and health packages, as do many private companies such as the UK-based Sun Modilex (tel: 0870 242 4211).

667246. Built in 1950, this luxury spot was renovated in the 1990s. It's slap bang on a broad section of the beach. Surfing, sailing school, steam baths, massage room. **$$**; **Iberostar Barlovento**, 1ra Ave e/ 10 y 12, tel: 045-667140; fax: 667254. New family holiday complex in Caribbean/ Spanish style with a seawater swimming pool. **$$**; **Dos Mares**, Calle 53 y 1ra Ave., tel: 045-612702; fax: 667495. Superb service in a friendly, 34-room hotel. It is easy to ignore the noise from the main road outside. **$$**; **Pullman**, Ave 1ra e/49 y 50, tel: 045-667161; fax: 667495. Simple, 16-room castle-style hotel in central position. Modernised in 2003. **$**.

Las Terrazas
La Moka, Complejo Turístico Las Terrazas, Autopista Habana – Pinar del Río, 51km (32 miles) from Havana, tel: 082-778600 or 07-204 3729. A well-established centre for ecotourists, with forest trees growing up between the split levels and patios. It has excellent service, a pool and footpaths. **$**.

Viñales
La Ermita, Ctra. de la Ermita, Viñales, 2km (1 mile), tel: 08-796071; fax: 336091. Hotel on top of hillside with beautiful panoramic view of the *mogotes*. **$$**; **Los Jazmines**, Ctra Pinar del Río, Viñales, 25km (16 miles), tel: 08-796205; fax: 08-796215. Colonial-style hotel with magnificent views of the *mogotes*. **$$**.

Cayo Levisa
Hotel Cayo Levisa, tel: 07-334238 or 08-756501; fax: 08-756505. Resort and diving centre on the beach, with 40 cabins. **$$**.

Maria La Gorda
Maria La Gorda Villa, tel: 082-

778131. Delightful hotel with 55 rooms next to the jetty and scuba centre. **$**.

Guamá

Guamá, Laguna del Tesoro, tel: 045-92535. Replica of a pre-Columbian village built over a lake. Modern amenities and persistent mosquitos. Currently being refurbished. **$**.

Bahía de los Cochinos

Playa Larga, Playa Larga, tel: 045-97225; fax: 94141. Basic cabins near a small beach and Revolution memorabilia. On the Zapata Peninsula. **$**.

Playa Girón

Playa Girón, tel: 045-94118; fax: 94117. An ugly hotel with 207 rooms and a pool. Next to good beach with facilities. **$$**.

Cienfuegos

Jagua, Calle 37 #1, tel: 0432-551003; fax: 551245. Destined to be a gambling casino when it was built in the 1950s, the Revolution intervened and it became a hotel. On the Punta Gorda peninsula 3km (2 miles) from the centre of the city. Renovated rooms, friendly atmosphere. **$$**; **Rancho Luna**, Ctra Rancho Luna, 16km (10 miles), tel: 043-548012 (Havana); fax: 548131. View over Jagua Bay and the sea. **$$**; **Faro Luna**, Ctra Rancho Luna, 18km (11 miles), tel: 043-548030; fax: 548062. A smaller resort next to Rancho Luna beach. **$**. **Pasacaballo**, Ctra Rancho Luna, 22km (14 miles), tel: 043-548013; fax: 548002. Fantastic view over Jagua fort and lighthouse. Good food, prompt service. **$**.

Trinidad

Ancón, Ctra María Aguilar, Playa Ancón, tel: 0419-6121 or 6123; fax: 6151. By a great beach. Best hotel in the area, if rather impersonal. **$$**; **Costasur**, Ctra María Aguilar, Playa María Aguilar, tel: 0419-6174; fax: 6173. Balconied rooms. If you are looking for peace and quiet, ask for a room away from the pool. Good food. **$$**.

Santiago de Cuba

Santiago de Cuba, Ave de las Américas y M, tel/fax: 022-687070. Luxury palace in post-modern style. Tennis courts, fitness studio, shopping centre, disco. **$$$**; **San Juan**, Ctra de Siboney, 1km (½ mile), tel: 0226-87200; fax: 687017. Simple, mid-range hotel in apartment style. Some 3.5km (2 miles) from the city centre. Swimming pool and bar. Lavish buffet meals; three-star rating. **$$**; **Casa Granda**, Lacret y Heredia, tel: 0226-86600. Grand hotel in the heart of Santiago, 58 rooms. **$$**; **Club Bucanero**, Ctra Baconao, 4km (2½ miles), Playa Arroyo de la Costa, tel: 022-686363; fax: 686070. Sports hotel with 200 simple rooms (sea or mountain view) with good facilities and all-inclusive price. **$$**; **Las Américas**, Ave Las Américas y General Cebreco, tel/fax: 022-642011. Small, simple city-centre hotel with swimming pool, 8km (5 miles) from airport. **$**.

Sierra Maestra

Brisas Sierra Mar, tel: 022-29110; fax: 29116. Mid-range hotel with good level of comfort. **$$**.

Gran Piedra National Park

Hotel Villa Gran Piedra, Ctra a Gran Piedra, 14.5km (9 miles), tel: 0226-86147. Comfortable but basic cabins with excellent views on a mountain ridge in the heart of the national park. Restaurant. **$**.

Bayamo

Sierra Maestra, Ctra Central km 1.5,

tel: 023-427970; fax: 427973. Simple hotel with swimming pool, in the hills to the east of Bayamo. **$**.

Baconao
Los Corales, Ctra Baconao, 10km (7 miles) from Baconao, Playa Cazonal, tel: 022-356121; fax: 356177. One hour from Santiago. Club style hotel. Shuttle bus to the watersports on Baconao beach. **$$**.

Baracoa
Porto Santo, Ctra al Aeropuerto, tel: 021-45105; fax: 45339. Set in a pretty location 0n a delightful bay, 3km (2 miles) from town. Excellent creole cuisine. **$$**.

Holguín
Mirador de Mayabe, Loma de Mayabe, Holguín, tel: 024-422160 or 425347, 10km (7 miles) from Holguín. Spectacular view over the Mayabe valley. Terrace pool. **$$**.

Guardalavaca and Playa Esmeralda
Sol Río de Luna, Ctra Holguín a Guardalavaca, Playa Esmeralda, tel: 024-30030; fax: 30035. This is a comfortable complex with good sporting facilities, diving centre, seafood restaurant and disco. **$$$**; **Sol Río de Mares**, Ctra Holguín a Guardalavaca, tel: 024-30060; fax: 30065. In the Naranjo Bay with yachting marina next door. **$$$**; **Atlántico**, Playa Guardalavaca, Banes, tel: 024-30180. On the beach offering good sporting facilities and a disco. **$$**. **La Brisas Hotel and Villas**, Playa Guardalavaca, Calle 2, Banes, tel: 24-30218; fax:30018. Imposing, modern hotel and villa complex with large swimming pool by the beach. **$$$**.

Isla de la Juventud
Colony, 41km (26 miles) from Nueva Gerona, tel: 046-398181; fax: 398420. All rooms with view of palm-tree garden and sea. Diving and squash (bring your own rackets). **$$**; **Villa Gaviotá**, Carretera La Fé km 1.5, outside Nueva Gerona, tel: 046-323256; fax: 324486. Small hotel with swimming pool near airport, but not for discerning travellers. **$**.

Cayo Largo
Pelícano, tel: 045-48333; fax: 48166. One of the best and newest hotels on the island. 224 rooms in the hotel, 110 in *cabañas*. Plenty of sporting facilities. **$$$**; **Isla del Sur**, tel: 045-48111–8; fax: 48201. Classified as a three-star hotel but, despite the clean and spacious rooms, is only awarded two. All-inclusive. **$$**; **Villa Capricho** (booking via Isla del Sur, in summer Pelícano; tel: 045 48111; fax: 48201). Air-conditioned rooms in palm-roofed *cabañas* close to the sea. **$$**.

Cayería del Norte
Blau Colonial Cayo Coco, Cayo Coco, tel: 033-301300; fax: 301389. A big, luxurious hotel set on a peninsula in the north of the island with small plazas, a 'town hall', parks, *bodegas*, piano bar and shopping arcade. Plus diving, snorkelling, water-skiing and horse-riding. **$$$**; **Meliá Cayo Coco**, Cayo Coco, tel: 033-301180; fax: 301195. An adults-only hotel. Opened in 2000 right on the beach, edged with palm trees. Rooms and bungalows. **$$$**; **Gran Club Santa Lucía**, Playa Santa Lucía, tel: 032-6109 or 6265. Spacious all-inclusive complex on broad, white-sand beach with beachside grill. **$$**; **Club Caracol**, Playa Santa Lucía, tel: 032-365158; fax: 365307. Hear the waves lapping on shore from the peaceful beachside bungalows, lacks atmosphere. **$**.

INDEX